W9-BZG-164

THE
SHAKER
COOKBOOK

Recipes and Lore from
the Valley of God's Pleasure

Caroline B. Piercy   Arthur P. Tolve

Illustrated by
Kathy Jakobsen and Patricia J. Forgac
Designed by Lynn Hostetler
General Editor: James H. Bissland III

WATERFORD PUBLIC LIBRARY

Gabriel's Horn Publishing Co.
Bowling Green, Ohio

3 3988 10081 4919

Gabriel's Horn Publishing Co.
P.O. Box 141
Bowling Green, Ohio 43402

An earlier version of this book was published as *The Shaker Cook
Book: Not by Bread Alone:* ©1953 by Caroline B. Piercy

Copyright renewed 1981 by Margaret P. Pierce and Carol P. Spohr

Renewal copyright assigned to The Shaker Historical Society

New recipe matter and Instructions ©1984 by Arthur P. Tolve

"Welcome to the Valley" ©1984 by James H. Bissland III

Front cover illustration ©1984 by Kathy Jakobsen

Back cover illustration and all inside illustrations ©1984 by Patricia
J. Forgac

All rights reserved. No part of this book may be duplicated, trans-
mitted or reproduced in any electronic or mechanical manner what-
soever – including with any photocopying, recording, or
information storage and retrieval system – without express written
permission from the appropriate copyright holder. Brief quotations
may be embodied in critical articles, reviews and news reports. For
information, write the publisher.

Printed in the United States of America.

99 98 97 96   14 13 12 11 10 9

ISBN 0-911861-02-5

THE SHAKER COOKBOOK

ABOUT THE COVER:

"North Union Shaker Village"
Oil on canvas, by Kathy Jakobsen
Copyright ©1984 Kathy Jakobsen
Courtesy of Jay Johnson Inc.

This 1984 painting by folk artist Kathy Jakobsen recreates the long-vanished Shaker community at North Union, Ohio, as it may have looked in the 1850s. The viewer is looking to the southwest, perhaps from the vantage point of the third floor of the Shakers' brick woolen mill. The buildings here are some of those of the Center Family, and include (left to right) the combined Office and Guest House, the Girls' House, the huge Dwelling House, a wood shed, and (in red) the Broom Shop, housing one of the community's principal industries. The buildings front on what is known today as Lee Road in Shaker Heights, a suburb of Cleveland. No Shaker buildings remain from the time when the area was known as "the Valley of God's Pleasure."

ILLUSTRATIONS IN THE TEXT:

Copyright ©1984 Patricia J. Forgac

The pen-and-ink illustrations found in the text and on the back cover were created for this book by Patricia J. Forgac, heritage director and assistant city planner for the city of Shaker Heights. Each chapter begins with a drawing of one of the buildings from the Shaker community of North Union. Scattered throughout the text are drawings of items in the collection of the Shaker Historical Society in Shaker Heights, some original to North Union and others from various Shaker societies.

*To the great host of Shaker "Kitchen Sisters" who
labored to please God in preparing the
viands entrusted to their hands*

CONTENTS

An Introduction

The Recipes

In Conclusion

ILLUSTRATIONS

NORTH UNION BUILDINGS

None of the original Shaker buildings remain today. These illustrations were drawn from old photographs.

SHAKER ARTIFACTS

All of the following items are in the collection of the Shaker Historical Society, in Shaker Heights, Ohio, site of the former North Union Shaker society.

ACKNOWLEDGEMENTS

by Caroline B. Piercy
(for the 1953 edition)

I am deeply grateful to:

The little old cookbook containing the Shaker recipes gleaned by my mother, for to it I owe my genuine interest in all things Shaker;

The Western Reserve Historical Society librarians who set before me abundant material in the form of Shaker household journals, travel records and diaries which have given me intimate glimpses into the everyday life at North Union;

Mrs. Jessie Haynes, of the Wayside Museums of Harvard, Massachusetts, who sent me old recipes from Canterbury Community;

Sister Ethel Peacock, of the Sabbathday Lake Shakers, who enlightened me on the subject of Shaker Applesauce and bread-making;

Sister Mildred Barker, of the Sabbathday Lake Shakers, for some recipes of sweetmeats for which that community has been famous – such chocolate mints! such preserves!

Sister Marguerite Frost, of the Canterbury Shakers, who most generously furnished me material on Shaker herb culture and some very flavorful recipes;

Mrs. Julius Zieget, of Peterboro, New Hampshire, and of Philadelphia, who introduced me to Sister Marguerite and also to her New England herb garden;

Sister Jennie Wells, of the Hancock Shakers in Massachusetts, for her far-famed rule for "Shaker potatoes";

Mr. William Harrison, director of Wayside Museums, for his reference to "The Story of the Shakers and Some of Their Cooking Recipes – Calendar for 1882-3," and to my doctor-husband who so patiently let me "try out" on him many of these dishes and who gave me invaluable pointers on nutrition – "the basic seven," calories, vitamins and minerals – and on the international or world-wide important position food holds today.

by Arthur P. Tolve
(for the 1984 revised edition)

I am appreciative of:

My wife Cecilia, in recognition of the lonely hours she spent, and for the many things we did and did not do while revising the recipes for this book;

My sisters-in-law for their testing of recipes, and their helpful suggestions on how to improve them.

by James H. Bissland III
(for the 1984 revised edition)

I am especially grateful to:

Allison Dunn for her enthusiasm and skill in testing the recipes, and all the Dunns for their critiquing of the results;

Mary Webb, a member of the Shaker Historical Society whose enthusiastic support from the beginning helped turn the idea for this edition into a reality; Virginia Atkinson, the talented director of the Shaker Historical Society, for her invaluable cooperation in making Museum resources available; Carl R. Withers, president of the Society, for facilitating the legal arrangements for the book; and past president Wallace N. Martel and other officers and members of the Society for their support for the idea of a new and revised eidtion of an out-of-print classic;

Frank and Sarah Breithaupt, a talented team of photographer and writer-editor, for providing valuable help when needed.

Joan, for her patience.

WELCOME TO THE VALLEY

The Center Family Dwelling House,
North Union, Ohio

WELCOME TO THE VALLEY
By James H. Bissland III

*We have been sent to take up our residence in the forest where we are laboring mightily
to minister the blessed Gospel of Mother to all souls who are willing to receive it, according
to our light and measure. – Elder Ashbel Kitchell*

Eight miles east of downtown Cleveland and about the same distance south
of Lake Erie is the city of Shaker Heights, a prosperous suburb of curving,
tree-shaded boulevards, handsome homes, and spacious parks. Before this
"garden city" suburb was developed early in the twentieth century, however,
another community existed here: the North Union society of Shakers, in a
locale they often referred to as the Valley of God's Pleasure.

The city may be the only one in the United States named for the
Shakers, but it is also one of the few places where Shakers lived for many
years and none of their buildings remain. Almost everything left by them was
swept away more than three-quarters of a century ago by the conversion of
their lands into a carefully planned suburb tied by rapid transit to the heart
of Cleveland. The preservation of their memory depends on organizations
like the city's Shaker Historical Society and efforts like this book.

Both the Society, which maintains a museum on what was once Center
Family land, and this book share a common parent. The late Caroline
Behlen Piercy, who was born in Cleveland only three years before the
Shakers left North Union, was a catalyst for forming the Shaker Historical
Society in 1947. And in 1953—only two years before her death—she published *The Shaker Cook Book: Not by Bread Alone*, the first modern collection
of authentic Shaker recipes. Her book was based primarily on recipes
gathered by her mother, a close friend of the North Union Shakers, as well
as other Shaker sources.

The book you are holding now—*The Shaker Cookbook: Recipes and Lore
from the Valley of God's Pleasure*—is a completely revised and redesigned
version of Mrs. Piercy's pioneering effort; in particular, the recipes have been
thoroughly tested and modified, where necessary, for the convenience of
modern cooks. The instructional and historical material has been edited,
expanded in some cases, and made more concise in others. And the illustrations are completely new: this book presents the most comprehensive view
yet of the buildings that vanished long ago from the Valley of God's Pleasure.

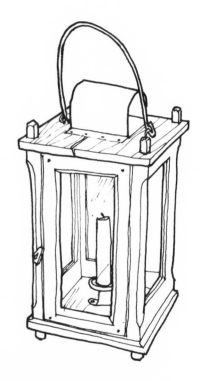

*Wooden lantern, the first gift to the
Shaker Historical Society.*

How did the Shakers come to the Valley of God's Pleasure—and why did they leave?

By the early 1800s, eleven Shaker communities had been established in New England and New York state. Ohio was still a developing frontier, secured from the Indians only in 1795. Into this pioneer region came Shaker missionaries. The first western society was established in 1805 at Turtle Creek in Warren County, near Cincinnati. Called Union Village, this society in turn spawned several offspring communities. Two were nearby in southwestern Ohio: Watervliet, established 1806, and Whitewater, about 1824.

A third, however, was established near the opposite corner of the state, primarily in the township of Warrensville near Cleveland. It all started with the visit to Union Village by Ralph Russell in 1821. Impressed with what he saw there, Russell returned to Warrensville, "a strong, clear ray of light" having led him all the way from Union Village to a spot near his dwelling. The zealous Russell soon converted several neighboring settlers, and when two elders arrived from Union Village the following spring, they found strong leadership and abundant land at the service of the church.

Reflecting its origins, the new community was called "the North Union." It thrived over the next three decades. The North Union society came to encompass 1,366 acres on the high tableland overlooking Cleveland. The land was gently rolling and divided by Doan Brook, which provided a shallow valley. The Shakers found the land better suited to dairying and grazing purposes than raising grain; large barns, spotlessly maintained, soon joined the other buildings serving the Believers.

Three economically self-sufficient Shaker "families" were established in the Valley of God's Pleasure. The largest, of about 100 men and women at its peak, was the Center or Middle Family, located in the vicinity of today's Lee Road and Shaker Boulevard. Among its three dozen structures were the huge Center Family Dwelling House (at the spot where Ralph Russell's column of light had touched), the Broom Shop (which housed a major North Union industry), the Woolen Mill (a three-story brick structure), the Meeting House, a hospital, school, and a combined office and guesthouse. Large orchards lay near the Center Family, as did a grove of mulberry trees and the Shaker burying ground.

A mile northwest of the Center Family was the Mill (or North) Family, situated at the end of a lake created by a Shaker dam. In addition to a dwelling house and the usual barns and service buildings, the Mill Family properties included both a sawmill and the famed Shaker Gristmill, described in its time as a marvel of engineering. With walls of stone four feet thick, the Gristmill rose two stories above the tableland and dropped four stories below it to the tail race.

About a half mile southeast of the Center Family was the Gathering (or East) Family. Here dwelt applicants to the Shakers, as well as "Winter Shakers" (persons who simply took refuge with the Shakers during hard times). Like the other families, the Gathering Family had its own dwelling house, barns, gardens and orchards.

The North Union Society appears to have reached the peak of its success in the 1850s, with membership variously estimated at two to three hundred. About 1858 North Union experienced a vaguely described financial problem, and the quality of leadership is said to have begun to slip. With the industrial boom and secularism that followed the Civil War, popular interest in Shakerism declined and it became harder for the sect to advance economically. Membership decreased: by 1870 there were about 125 persons at North Union and rumors of a shutdown were circulating. The population was down to 102 by 1875; the Gristmill was described as having "failed for years to be more than a convenience," and the buildings were beginning to show signs of neglect.

Lacking a sufficient number of younger members, it was increasingly necessary to hire outside help. In 1886 the proud old Gristmill was destroyed for quarrying purposes. By 1889, the population had declined to twenty-seven persons and it was decided by the central ministry at Mt. Lebanon to close North Union, moving the remaining members to Union Village and Watervliet, Ohio. The society's furniture was sold at auction that year; the land and buildings were sold three years later. Most of the buildings sank into decay and slowly, one by one, began to disappear; the process was completed with the launching of the modern development of Shaker Heights by the Van Sweringen brothers in 1905. Today, the memory of the North Union Shakers is maintained by the Shaker Historical Society in a museum and library at 16740 South Park Boulevard, Shaker Heights.

North Union was not the first Shaker community to close, nor was it the last. At their peak, the Believers had eighteen major communities (plus shorter lived ones at six other locations); one after another most have had to close.

And yet, more than two centuries after Mother Ann reached these shores, two Shaker communities, with a handful of members, remain even today: one at Canterbury, New Hampshire, and the other at Sabbathday Lake, Maine. Both are open to visitors during the travel season. Year by year, popular interest in the Shakers grows, and so does admiration for what they contributed to the American experience: idealism, and devotion, ingenuity, thrift, humanity, reverence for nature.

Though their numbers are few, the remaining Shakers are not concerned at their decrease. As Sister R. Mildred Barker of Sabbathday Lake told members of the Shaker Historical Society on a visit to the Valley of God's Pleasure a few years ago:

"Shakerism is no failure. It is good, and therefore of God, and no good is ever a failure.

"The principles and ideals which the Shakers were the first to expound have gone out into the world and, like a pebble dropped in the water, we cannot measure the distance of the influence they have borne....Shakerism is not dying out, nor is it a failure."

A FORETASTE

The Center Family Girls' House,
North Union, Ohio

A FORETASTE
by *Caroline B. Piercy*

We believe that we are debtors to God in relation to one another and that we are to improve our time and our talents in this life in that manner in which we are most useful. – Shaker Covenant.

This little volume on Shaker cookery may never find its way into the technology departments of our large libraries where legions of cookbooks stand in neat rows, for I am writing it not for its scientific contribution, but rather to set forth the Shakers' important contributions to the development of an all-American cookery.

I was asked to prepare a booklet on Shaker cookery for the Shaker Historical Society of Shaker Heights (near Cleveland), Ohio. I became fascinated by the project, not just because many of the recipes were unique and deserved preservation, but because of the attitude of this religious order toward food and its preparation. According to the Shaker belief, work and worship are intertwined: "Give your hands to work and your hearts to God" is their well-known motto.

The Shakers, or United Society of Believers in Christ's Second Appearing as they also called themselves, believed their sole purpose in life was to establish God's kingdom here on earth. Their hands, their minds, their hearts were wholly dedicated to that end, and their vast kitchens and numerous workshops were as sacred to them as were their meeting houses and assembly halls. Whether they were making luscious pies, dumplings and dainty flummeries, or beautifully crafted wooden household utensils and fine skeins of yarn and flax, the Shakers put into their work what their religion taught: that man was put into this world in order to establish "Heavens on earth" where peace, brotherly love and honesty reigned.

For material for my booklet on Shaker cookery I turned to a well-finger-marked manuscript cook book that had stood on our pantry shelf when I was a very small child. This volume had always fascinated me, for on its blue-lined pages were written in my mother's dainty Spencerian script recipes for Eldress Clymena's Blue Flower Omelets, Sister Abigail's Strawberry Flummery and Sister Content's Herb Butter for supper sandwiches and spread on freshly cooked vegetables. Such mouth-watering suggestions! And there many other neatly penned rules for crunchy Sugar Cookies, Molasses Taffy, Rose Petal Sweetmeats and Maple Creams bulging with the rich meats of butternuts. What gave the little book its special aura was that whenever my

Small tin butter churn, 22½" high. This was a pump churn, agitated by moving the handle up and down.

mother and I used these time-honored recipes, she would tell me how she gleaned this rare collection. It all resulted from her many visits as a child and later as a young woman to "The Valley of God's Pleasure," commonly known as the North Union Shaker Society, about a mile from her former home near Cleveland.

This peaceful community, she would tell me, "was without jail, without poor, without saloons, nor did they learn the art of war therein. These devout Shakers loved one another as brothers and sisters. They withdrew from the world in order to establish villages throughout our young nation, where the Golden Rule was the one law by which they lived."

How I longed to know these devout souls! It stimulated my youthful imagination to think of the Sisters endlessly preparing delicious food for their enormous households, and not looking upon it as a labor, but as a glorious opportunity to serve God joyously by feeding His children. As we concocted a Shaker apple pie, delicately flavored with rosewater, from the pages of this enchanting cookbook, my mother would tell me how her father had arranged for the skilled brethren to mill the timber and grain of their large acreage, and to have their apples converted into the famed Shaker cider at their presses. There, also, her family brought their brooms, vats, barrels, kegs, firkins and noggins, wooden pails and mammoth washtubs. The butter, lard, cheese and eggs, as well as the applesauce and other preserves consumed by this large family were purchased from Deacon Daniel, the Shaker peddler who made his weekly rounds with a covered wagon crammed to the ribs with faultless Shaker produce.

In the sisters' knitting shop my mother's family bought the creamy-white and ruby-red yarns for the stockings, mittens, mufflers and fascinators (scarves) they needed throughout the long winters. And they bought countless baskets from the Believers, whose skilled fingers fashioned containers for every conceivable use, from picking berries to gathering firewood in the nearby forest. There were wide, sturdy clothes baskets that held a dozen freshly tubbed sheets, cheese baskets always bleached white from the whey, and tiny sewing baskets woven as smooth as velvet for fine needlecraft.

Here at these Shaker villages my mother became acquainted with the excellence of Shaker cookery, for hospitality reigned in these "Kingdoms of God on earth." Seldom was she allowed to leave North Union or the Valley of God's Pleasure without breaking bread—and such bread!—with some of the sisters. Often she would come away with one or many of the Shakers' tested recipes, which she would copy into the blue-lined pages of her notebook. The little volume contained more than rules for food. Its recipes were flavored with consecration and with a zeal for perfection, for whatever a Shaker undertook to accomplish she consecrated her entire being to its fulfillment. Whether it was the making of a pie or herb-laden soufflé or the erecting of a house of worship, Shaker hands were equally devoted to the task and they never ceased to seek better ways and means of performing their allotted duties.

Who were these Shakers and where did they come from? This religious sect originated about 1747 among a group of English Quakers who had been strongly influenced by a group of French religious refugees. In their meditation the English Quakers would tremble, which might lead to shaking, singing and shouting. Among this group who worshipped in Manchester, England, arose a young woman, Ann Lee, daughter of a blacksmith. Because of her great spiritual power and insight, she was accepted as the second embodiment of the Christ spirit upon earth by the "Shaking Quakers." Her followers called her Mother Ann.

The Shakers were persecuted in England. In 1774 Mother Ann and seven of her followers came to America where it had been revealed to her they would re-establish the Apostolic Church. Arriving at the outbreak of the American Revolution, the little band of unknown Britishers at first met with some hostility and little success. But in the closing years of the Revolution a religious revival broke out on the frontier. Word began to spread that in the wilderness above Albany—in Niskayuna—there dwelt a strange little band of Believers who were attempting to re-establish the early Christian Church; that they lived by the Golden Rule and patterned their lives wholly upon that of Jesus Christ, living celibate lives, sharing all they possessed, and being complete pacifists. Pilgrims traveled there. And Mother Ann traveled throughout New England.

Within a few years Mother Ann and the original little band of English Shakers had gone to their rest, but hundreds of converts had joined the ranks of the Believers in Christ's Second Appearing, and eleven Shaker communities had been established in Maine, New Hampshire, Connecticut, Massachusetts and New York. The movement spread west and south to establish four communities in Ohio and two in Kentucky (as well as short-lived ventures in Indiana, Georgia and Florida); at its peak strength in the mid-1800s the Shakers had eighteen communities and perhaps five thousand members. The typical Shaker community or "society" was divided into several economically independent "families" of one hundred or so members each.

Thus, the Shaker movement blossomed in the formative years of the Federal period. Adventure and experiment were the order of the day. Foreign dress, foods and wine were rapidly discarded in favor of native homespuns, home-brews and native ciders. The First Lady of the Land, Martha Washington, advocated the cultivation and development of an all-American cookery. With an almost unlimited resources of unturned sod and uncut virgin forests, the young country had what seemed at the time an inexhaustible supply of game and wild foods. And from the beginning the settlers of this new land had found many new foods awaiting them, such as Indian maize (corn), sweet potatoes, certain beans, pumpkins, squash, many new varieties of berries and wild plums and cranberries. All this profusion of new foods led to new dishes, new ways of cooking and a diet with a distinctive American flavor.

In this young nation teeming with activity—trying out this and that in an attempt to establish an independent American way of life—the Shakers played an important role. In the Shaker communities from Maine to Kentucky, the streets of the Believers were soon lined with buildings of excellent architecture. These buildings were equipped with furniture of their own making, designed for utility and durability. Their fields were vast and well cultivated and their orchards and vineyards soon stretched off at great distances. Well-tilled vegetable and herb gardens skirted each Shaker family's kitchen where substantial meals for a hundred brethren and sisters were prepared three times daily.

Butter churn in old red paint, 27" high.

Because of the religious zeal and integrity of the Shakers, their communties thrived remarkably and soon became models of thrift and high standards of living. Dedicating everything they did to their religion, the Shakers were thorough and exact in whatever they undertook, and they were always seeking better ways and means of performing the Herculean tasks of clearing and cultivating the land and harvesting their vast crops. They became inventors and produced countless gadgets, tools and machinery to increase their efficiency in production. They invented a rotary harrow, a threshing machine, a fertilizer spreader, a splint-cutting machine for the manufacture of baskets and boxes, a better windmill, an improved word-burning stove, a pea sheller, a butter churn driven by water power, a self-acting cheese press, an apple parer, a revolving oven and many other labor-saving devices. They seldom applied for patents on their inventions, for they considered such restrictions "as smacking of monopoly" which was contrary to the Golden Rule.

Their various communities being under the leadership of the central ministry in New York state at Mt. Lebanon (known as New Lebanon until 1861), all the communities shared in these improvements of field, factory and kitchen through constant visits and communication with each other. Thus, all their communities were soon in advance of their neighbors in production methods. The Shakers were also skilled horticulturists, developing new and better species of apples, plums and peaches. Moreover, they conducted the first nurseries in their localities. They were also pioneers in raising, packaging and distributing garden seeds in America. This called for scientific methods of selection from only the thriftiest plants. They produced leaflets on how to plant the seeds and how to cook and prepare the food grown. Again, the Shakers carried on the first large-scale production of kitchen and medicinal herbs and widely distributed information concerning their proper use. They improved their herds and flocks by importing and breeding thoroughbred stock. They observed high standards of sanitation in their vast barns and dairies when bacteria were yet unheard of and milk was often dangerously infected by unsanitary conditions.

Moreover, the Believers applied almost scientific methods in their cooking, for in working with vast amounts of food, exact weights and measures and relative amounts had to be estimated and established in a day when their contemporaries added typically added "a dash of this and a glob of that" in making their favorite dishes. Cooking for a hundred hungry mouths thrice daily demanded definite rules and exact measurements. Again, the Shakers recorded the works of their hands and left us definite information on cookery in a day when books on the art of cooking were few. In the large Shaker literature there is but one printed cookbook. This was written by Sister Mary Whitcher, and entitled *The Shaker House-Keeper*. However, in the manuscript annals of the various communities there are countless recipes used by these pioneer Americans.

The Shakers had an effect upon our national diet through their interest in vegetarianism. In the late 1830s a ban which lasted twelve years was placed on the use of meat throughout Shakerdom. Green vegetables, fruits, cereals, eggs, cheese and dairy products were substituted at a time when heavy meat diets, salt pork and corn were the accepted foods of the day. It was at this period that due to a lack of hostelries, the western Shaker societies served thousands of meals to the hosts of Easterners who migrated west by the hundreds. Enticed by the abundance of good food and comfortable lodgings, many a western trek ended within the Shaker gates. "We came seeking food and shelter, kind Elder, never realizing that the gates of eternal salvation would be opened up to us," was the frequent reward for Shaker hospitality.

Another strong influence these communities had on American cooking was achieved through their serving as the orphanages of that day. One might say they were the forerunner of the domestic science or home economics schools of a later period, for every girl raised by the order received along with her book-learning a thorough education in housewifery. Elder Frederick Evans, one of the Shakers' greatest spokesmen, stated that hundreds of such Shaker-trained young women went forth into the world when they became of age, thoroughly equipped to conduct a well-run household.

Probably the farthest-reaching Shaker influence on American cookery was through their success in the canning industry. The records show that they distributed thousands upon thousands of items of preserved food to markets as far distant as New Orleans. Each item was carefully inspected and labeled before it passed beyond the Shaker gates. The high standard of quality possessed by their goods created a great demand among the public for Shaker products. The Shaker label was a mark of their integrity on any item which bore their name.

In a day when calories and vitamins were yet unheard of, the Shaker sisters, because of their abhorrence of waste, used their "pot-licker," water in which certain vegetables had been cooked, in making gravies, stews and soups. They scrubbed their vegetables and usually boiled them in their peels, a method which we know is approved of today, for it conserves valuable nutrition. At their semi-weekly social meetings, articles from the New York papers and from science journals which pertained to agriculture, food, nutrition and hygeine were read and freely discussed. From 1871 through 1899 the Shakers published their own magazine; although it appeared under various titles it is usually referred to as *The Manifesto*. A special column entitled "Home Topics" contained recipes and household hints. This magazine had a fairly wide distribution among "the World People" as well as among all the Shaker communities. Again, *The Manifesto* had many items about diet and its relation to health.

The Shakers' great kitchens were built for communal living and were equipped with conveniences often years ahead of the times—running water, stone sinks, specially built ranges and ovens, such as the revolving pie oven at Canterbury planned so that heat was evenly distributed and the baked loaves and confections could most easily be removed by rotating the oven shelves. Cleanliness was almost a part of the Shaker creed. Mother Ann often remarked: "There is no dirt or filth in Heaven," and since the Shakers sought to establish "Heavens on Earth," their communities were kept, as near as possible, spotless. The great kitchens and pantries were lined with innumerable cupboards and drawers "where everything had its place and was kept in its place" according to Mother Ann's admonitions. To add further to the efficiency of these kitchens there was always a cooking kitchen and a baking kitchen. In the high-ceilinged, well-ventilated cellar, close to the fruit and vegetable bins, was the canning kitchen especially equipped with great ranges, sufficient tables and tremendous copper kettles which could turn bushels of raw food into rare sauces and condiments for the long winter ahead. It was in these canning kitchens that American mass production first saw the light of day.

Like Shaker architecture, furniture and dress, the Believers' cooking exhibited genuine simplicity and good quality. The Shakers abhorred shoddy work, adulteration and useless ornamentation. All their work was colored and inspired by Mother Ann's simple truths, such as, "Labor to make the ways of God your ways." Concerning cooking she advised the sisters: "See that your victuals are prepared in good order and on time so that when the Brethren return from their labors in the fields, they can bless you and eat their food with thankfulness, without murmuring, and thereafter be able to worship in the beauty of holiness."

The sisters understood that the planning, preparing and serving of meals was a great responsibility and a great service to God, for on this task depended the health, comfort and well-being of the large families. The brethren hungry from toil in the fields and workshop, the growing children from their small tasks, the aged Believers, all gathered about the long trestled tables three times daily looking for sustenance, satisfaction and fellowship. It was this conviction of the Shaker sister, that in her hands had been placed a task into which she must put all the wisdom and skill with which God had endowed a Shaker woman, that earned for Shaker cookery the high praise from all who partook of their wholesome, delicious fare. These faithful laborers in the kitchens of the Valley of God's Pleasure keenly realized that man does not live by bread alone.

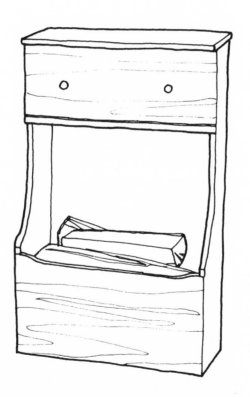

Wood box, 5' high, with drawer at top for storing kindling. Sold at the North Union dispersal auction in 1889, it eventually was given to the Shaker Society as a gift by the son of the purchasers.

INSTRUCTIONS

The Mill Family Spring House (left), Dwelling House (center),
and Cheese House

INSTRUCTIONS
by Arthur P. Tolve

See that your victuals are prepared in good order and on time so that when the Brethren return from their labors in the fields, they can bless you and eat their food with thankfulness, without murmuring, and thereafter be able to worship in the beauty of holiness.
– Mother Ann Lee.

For delicate, natural flavors of Shaker recipes, use the freshest and purest of ingredients. Some ingredients used by the Shakers are not readily available today, but recipes in *The Shaker Cookbook* have been carefully revised for the convenience of modern cooks. For example, the milk found in most supermarkets can't compare with the thick, rich milk the "Kitchen Sisters" obtained direct from the Shaker barns. For similar results in cooking, therefore, half-and-half or light cream has been substituted in those recipes dependent on the fat content of milk. Unsalted butter made from fresh, sweet cream will yield best results when butter is specified, since most of the butter offered for sale today has been made from sour cream. When it is available, the quality and flavor of unsalted "tub butter" is ideal.

The eggs used by the Shakers were of the freshest quality, since they were gathered and used the same day. For modern cooks, extra-large brown-shelled eggs are recommended for the deepest egg-color, although excellent results may be obtained with white-shelled eggs as well. Remember that eggs, as with any protein food, require low heat to cook. High heat toughens egg protein and causes a discoloration of the yolk. In recipes requiring chopped, cooked eggs, do not boil them; cook them in water at the simmering point or slightly below.

Athough fresh produce is available to us throughout the year, quality may vary according to the time it spends in storage and the handling it must endure. On the other hand, today's marketplace offers a variety and convenience undreamed of by the early Shakers. When good fresh produce is unavailable, the frozen ingredient may be substituted with good results, exercising care to obtain the variety that most closely resembles fresh.

Most meats, fish and poultry available in the better supermarkets or butcher shops will provide a satisfactory finished product. However, prepackaged products tend to become watery, especially after being displayed for long periods of time, and frozen products undergo a texture change when thawed and then cooked.

In the recipes that call for baking powder, the double-acting variety

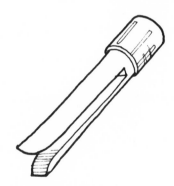

Clothespin, North Union. The wooden clothespin is said to be a North Union invention.

produces consistently good results. Pure and natural flavoring extracts, not artificial, are recommended for the best-tasting products.

Flour should be obtained with the intended use in mind. For example, soft-wheat cake flour should be used for most cakes and some cookies; hard-wheat bread flour produces the finest results for most yeast-raised breads. The cake flour produces a smooth-textured product, with a light, velvety crumb, while the high-protein bread flour produces an elastic framework which results in high, light breads. General-utility all-purpose flour is suited for use in most other baked products, including quick breads and pastry, and as the thickening agent in most sauces. Sweet doughs, from which coffee cakes and sweet rolls are made, require all-purpose flour or a mixture of three parts of bread flour to one part of cake flour.

Granulated sugar should be used unless otherwise specified, but brown sugar will produce comparable results in most cases, with a delicate variation in flavor. Since maple sugar is not readily available, brown or granulated-white sugar has been substituted in *The Shaker Cookbook,* and maple flavoring has been substituted to produce the traditional flavor. Maple syrup, which has been substituted for the maple sugar and some of the liquid, did not harm the integrity of the finished product.

Fresh herbs produce an unmistakably superior product than do dried, but fresh are not always available. If dried herbs must be used, substitute only one-third for the amount required of the fresh. Also, commercially available dried leaf-herbs usually contain stems which can impart a bitterness to the finished product. When using herbs, moderation is the key. The flavor of the herb in the finished product should be subtle and mild, not overbearing.

MEASUREMENTS: Standard measuring utensils, used correctly, help assure consistent quality. Remember to use liquid measuring utensils for measuring liquid ingredients and dry measuring utensils for measuring dry ingredients.

Measurements of all ingredients should be level. To measure dry ingredients, heap the ingredient and level evenly with the edge of a cake spatula. Stainless steel or aluminum dry measuring utensils are not affected by heat or improper handling, but high-impact plastic, while versatile, may not be heat resistant. Liquid ingredients require leveling also, but the liquid in the utensil should appear to be resting on the utensil's measuring line. Therefore, the utensil should be transparent. A tempered glass utensil is heat-resistant and does not change shape as readily as plastic. Avoid using the so-called "combination" measuring utensils; measurements are usually not accurate and results may be dissapointing.

Flour should always be sifted before measuring. It can be sifted directly into the measuring utensil or heaped in afterward with a spatula, but in either case be sure to level the flour with the edge of a spatula. Do not shake the sifted flour while measuring or the air incorporated in it during sifting will be lost. Granulated sugar, if lumpy, should be sifted before measuring, but brown sugar should be packed firmly into the dry measuring utensil to remove air pockets and then leveled with the edge of a spatula. Because syrups and frostings are thick and viscous and tend to heap in the center of the utensil, level them off evenly after heaping in a dry measuring utensil. Oils should be poured into liquid measuring utnesils, with care taken that the measurement is level and even. Melted butter should also be measured in this manner. Be sure to scrape the side of the measuring utensil to remove any clinging oil. Eggs when used singly, should be of the extra-large size. With quantities, measure the eggs in liquid measuring cupfuls, counting each cupful as the equivalent of 4 jumbo or extra-large eggs, or 5 large eggs, or 6 medium eggs, or 7 small eggs.

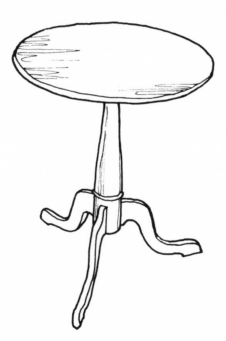

Shaker candlestand.

SOUPS

The Woolen Mill, Center Family,
North Union, Ohio

SOUPS

*Every day is Thanksgiving Day at the Shaker communities for the Believers never cease
being thankful for the great bounty God bestows upon His children.*
– A North Union elder.

In the early days at North Union and probably at the other western Shaker communities, the great iron soup pot was kept handy by the constantly glowing fire and into it went the trimmings of meat, bones of roasts and the broth from all their cooked vegetables. At the end of the day this broth was drained and used in the making of stews and gravy on the morrow. However, lamb and mutton seldom went into this pot for they are too strong in flavor, while pork is too rich and sweet to make good stock.

Like all good cooks, the Shaker kitchen sisters classified soups into three groups: *thin, clear soups* which stimulate appetite and are known as consommé, bouillon and broth; *thin cream soups* called bisques and vegetable broths; and *heavy, thick soups* and *chowders*.

Soups need never become a commonplace dish, for the garnishes and the accompanying crackers, croutons, breadsticks, toasts and cheese straws challenge any cook's imagination. It is amazing to read what all the Shaker sisters converted into soups, broths and chowders.

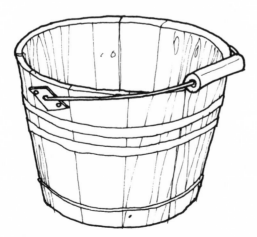

Wooden water pail from Sabbathday Lake.

Shaker Beef Broth

2 ox-tails
OR 3 pounds neck of beef
1 knuckle of veal
1 gallon cold water
1 tablespoon salt
12 peppercorns, bruised
2 carrots, quartered
4 parsnips
4 ribs celery with leaves
½ cup flat-leaf parsley
4 green onions or scallions with tops
¼ teaspoon mace
2 bay leaves
1 sprig thyme

Place meat and bones in soup pot and add water. Let stand 1 hour. The veal knuckle adds body (gelatine) to the broth and imparts a rich flavor. Place over moderate heat and bring to the boiling point. Skim well. Reduce heat and simmer gently for 3½ hours. Add vegetables, herbs and seasonings. Simmer 30 minutes and strain through 5 layers of cheesecloth. Refrigerate 24 hours and remove all fat from the surface.

Eldress Clymena Miner, North Union

White or Veal Stock

4 pounds veal knuckle and shank
Necks and feet of 2 chickens
4 quarts cold water
2 medium onions, quartered
2 carrots, quartered
1 rib celery
1 parsnip, quartered
12 sprigs flat-leaf parsley
1 sprig thyme
2 bay leaves
12 peppercorns, bruised
1 tablespoon salt
¼ teaspoon mace

Skin chicken feet by scalding first. If chicken feet are unavailable, substitute 2 tablespoons plain gelatine. Place veal and chicken parts in soup pot with cold water and let stand 1 hour. Place pot over low heat and bring to the boiling point. Reduce heat and simmer very gently for 3½ hours, skimming surface foam frequently. Do not boil. Add onions, carrots, celery, parsley and seasoning and simmer gently for another half hour. Strain through a colander, reserving meat for other use. Refrigerate for 12 hours before clearing.

Variation: If brown stock is desired, heat oven to 500°F. Place meat and bones (not poultry) in a greased shallow pan. Place in oven until lightly browned. Toss vegetables and seasonings with meat and bones and return to oven to become dark brown. Continue as for white stock, cleansing drippings in the baking pan with water and adding it to the stock pot.

To Clear or Clarify Stock: Remove fat layer from surface of cold stock. Heat just enough to melt jellied stock. Measure, and for each quart of stock, break in 3 eggs, including shells, and whisk thoroughly to combine. Bring to a rolling boil and boil 5 minutes. Strain immediately through 6 layers of cheesecloth. Poultry stock rarely, if ever, becomes crystal-clear.

Sister Lottie's Chicken Soup

Simmer chicken in water for about 3 hours. Remove chicken and reserve stock. Remove meat from bones and cut into small cubes. Discard bones and skin and reserve meat. Place bay leaf and peppercorns in an herb bag. Dice fennel or anise. If fresh fennel or anise is unavailable, substitute celery and add 1 teaspoon anise seed to herb bag. Add onion, anise stalks, herb bag, salt and rice to reserved stock. Simmer slowly until rice is tender. Remove herb bag and add chicken meat and parsley to soup. Reheat to simmering and serve immediately. Makes six servings.

4-pound fowl, disjointed
2½ quarts water
6 peppercorns
1 bay leaf
2 stalks fresh fennel or anise
1 small onion, minced
1 teaspoon salt
⅔ cup converted rice
1 tablespoon minced parsley

Spring Vegetable Soup

Wash potatoes and carrots. Slice thinly, but do not peel. Melt butter and add leeks, celery and parsley. Sauté until vegetables are translucent, but not brown. Blanch the green pepper and lettuce in boiling water for 1 minute. Heat broth and pour over vegetables including raw potato and carrot. Season with salt and pepper if desired, and simmer slowly for 20 minutes. Serve hot with toasted crackers. Serves 4 to 6.

Amelia's Shaker Recipes

2 raw potatoes
1 raw carrot
1 tablespoon butter
2 leeks or 4 green onions, sliced
3 ribs celery
3 sprigs flat-leaf parsley
2 parsnips
¼ cup green pepper, chopped
1 cup shredded lettuce
2 quarts chicken broth

Shaker Fresh Herb Soup

Melt butter in an enameled, glass or stainless steel saucepan. Add herbs and celery and sauté for 3 minutes. Add broth and seasonings. Simmer gently for 20 minutes. Place slices of toast in a tureen and pour soup over them. Add nutmeg and sprinkle with grated cheese. Serve very hot. Serves 4 to 6. Amelia's Shaker Recipes

Note: If dried herbs are to be used, decrease quantity by ⅔ and tie them in a cheesecloth herb bag. Remove herb bag before serving.

1 tablespoon butter
2 tablespoons chives, chopped
2 tablespoons chervil, minced
2 tablespoons sorrel, minced
½ teaspoon tarragon, cut fine
1 cup celery, minced
1 quart chicken broth
Salt and pepper to taste
½ teaspoon sugar
6 slices toast
1/16 teaspoon nutmeg
Grated cheddar cheese

Eldress Clymena's Tomato Soup

24 medium tomatoes, ripe
2 ribs celery, diced
2 tablespoons green pepper, minced
2 bay leaves
1 teaspoon salt
1 teaspoon sugar
1/16 teaspoon cayenne pepper
1 tablespoon parsley, minced
1/4 teaspoon onion juice
1/2 teaspoon lemon juice
1/2 cup lightly salted whipped cream
OR sour cream

Do not skin tomatoes, but cut into quarters and place in a heavy enameled, glass or stainless steel pot with celery, green pepper and bay leaves. Cover tightly and simmer 20 minutes without adding any water. Pass through a sieve to remove skin and seeds and return to pot. Add seasonings and bring to boiling point. Pour into heated bowls and top with whipped cream or sour cream. Serves 6.

Oyster Stew

2 pints oysters
4 tablespoons butter
1 teaspoon salt
1/4 teaspoon white pepper
2 cups milk
2 cups heavy cream
1 tablespoon minced parsley

Place oysters and their liquid in an enameled, glass or stainless steel sauce-pan. Add butter and seasonings. Stew over very low heat for 12 minutes, stirring frequently. Add milk and cream and simmer until oysters curl slightly at the edges. Sprinkle top with the minced parsley and serve from a heated tureen immediately. Toasted soda or oyster crackers go well with this soup. Serves 6 to 8.

Mary Whitcher's Shaker House-Keeper

HINTS FOR SHAKER SOUPS: All heavy fats should be trimmed from meats and fowls before they go into the soup pot, for fats flatten the flavor of soups.

Skimming soup during cooking is very important if you wish a fine clear broth.

Broths may be made from fresh meat or fish, or from roast bones or turkey carcasses, but the latter will not make a clear broth and should be used only as a base for cream soups.

HOW WELCOME SPRING WAS: Today we cannot imagine what it meant to the early Shakers to taste the first green sprouts after their long winter diet of root vegetables, dried corn and salt meats. Because the first green sprouts were so scarce and precious, they very often went into the soup pot, there to be stretched into plenty for the large household.

Mary Whitcher's Okra Soup

4 pounds veal shank, cracked
2 large onions, diced
2 carrots, diced
4 tomatoes, skinned and cut
4½ quarts water
1 teaspoon salt
½ teaspoon sugar
⅛ teaspoon pepper
1 quart fresh okra, thinly sliced
OR 20 ounces frozen okra, cut

Place knuckles in an enameled, glass or stainless steel soup pot with all vegetables except okra. Add water and seasonings. Simmer over low heat for 6½ hours. Remove meat and cartilage from knuckles and cut into small pieces. Return to pot with soup and add okra. Simmer 30 minutes. This okra soup equals any turtle soup. Serve hot. Makes 8 servings.

According to Mary Whitcher, "This soup is a meal in itself and should not be served with a dinner but as a supper (or luncheon) dish along with some greens and a hearty dessert."

THE STORY OF MARY WHITCHER: With her husband, Benjamin, Mary Whitcher was living on a hundred-acre ancestral farm in New Hampshire when in 1782 they were converted by two Shaker missionaries from New Lebanon. For ten years the Whitchers gathered Shaker converts under their hospitable roof, which was converted into the Canterbury Shaker community in 1792. (That community continues to this day, and is open to visitors from mid-May through mid-October.) Benjamin became the elder of this first family or unit and Mary was chosen as one of the trustees. Her small booklet, *Mary Whitcher's Shaker House-Keeper*, was first published about 1882 and has since become very rare.

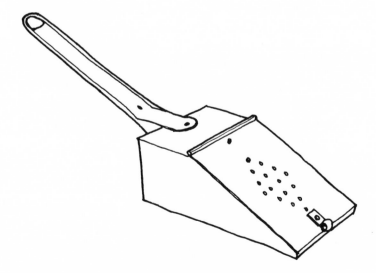

Tin ember box with pieced tin lid from Enfield, Connecticut.

Mock Turtle Soup

2 pounds veal knuckle, cracked
½ cup butter
1 carrot, diced
2 small onions, diced
1 rib celery, diced
2 whole cloves
1 bay leaf
½ cup flour
2 quarts White Stock (see Index)
1 cup tomato puree
3 cups cubed meat from White Stock
1 cup dry sherry
2 sprigs thyme
2 sprigs marjoram
Salt and pepper to taste
2 slices lemon
¼ teaspoon Tobasco
1 hard-cooked egg, chopped

Place knuckle in roasting pan with butter, carrot, onions, celery, cloves, bay leaf and roast to a light brown in a 500°F oven. Add flour and toss to mix well. Roast 20 minutes longer. Remove mixture to an enameled, glass or stainless steel soup pot. Cleanse drippings in the roasting pan with stock to deglaze and add to mixture in soup pot with stock and tomato puree. Simmer 3 hours. Strain. In a saucepan or skillet, combine meat, sherry and seasonings and cook slowly 10 minutes. Add strained stock mixture to the meat mixture and sprinkle surface with egg. Serve at once. Makes 8 servings.

NOTE: If dried herbs are used, allow ½ teaspoon each.

Old Fashioned Potato Soup

4 pounds small potatoes
2 tablespoons caraway seed
2 teaspoons salt
2 quarts water
6 green onions or small leeks, chopped
2 quarts light cream
2 tablespoons marjoram, chopped
1 teaspoon paprika
6 strips crisp bacon, minced

Scrub the potatoes, but do not peel. Place in an enameled, glass or stainless steel soup pot with caraway seed, salt and water. Simmer slowly for 30 minutes. Remove potatoes, peel and dice. Replace into pot with liquor in which they were cooked. Add green onions and simmer slowly 30 minutes. Pass through a coarse sieve or food mill, or process in a food processor until smoother but still fairly coarse. Return to pot, add cream and heat. Add marjoram and paprika. Garnish with bacon. Serve with toasted crackers. Makes 8 servings.

NOTE: If dried marjoram is used, add 1 teaspoon with green onion.

Mary Whitcher's Shaker House-Keeper

SABBATH FARE: Since the Shaker Sabbath started at sundown on Saturday, as little cooking as possible was done then and on Sunday. Such dishes as pease porridge, baked beans and puddings which improved with long baking in the great brick ovens were favorite Sabbath food in the early days.

Place corn in water and boil 5 minutes. Add salt, pepper and sugar. Melt butter in saucepan and blend in flour to form a roux. Slowly stir in cream to make a white sauce. Add corn mixture and the whole onion. Simmer slowly for 10 minutes. Remove onion and serve very hot with crisp crackers. Serves 6.

Mary Whitcher's Shaker House-Keeper

Place peas in cold water to cover. Refrigerate overnight. Drain well and simmer in stock for 2 hours. Add vegetables and seasonings and simmer slowly another 30 minutes. Pass through a coarse sieve or a food mill, or process in a food processor until smoother but still fairly coarse. Serve very hot with well-buttered rye bread croutons. Makes 4 servings.

Place beans in cold water to cover and refrigerate overnight. Drain and add to ham bone and water and simmer slowly until beans are tender. Add vegetables and cook another 20 minutes. Remove bone and pass soup through a sieve or a food mill. Season to taste and add minced parsley. Serve very hot with fried bread fingers. Serves 6 to 8. North Union

VARIATION: For variety in texture, do not puree soup, but leave beans whole.

NOTE: If ham bone is unavailable, make a broth from 2 smoked ham hocks and 3½ quarts water. Simmer 2 to 3 hours, or pressure cook 30 minutes.

Fresh Corn Soup

2 cups corn, freshly scraped from the cob
2 cups water
1 teaspoon salt
⅛ teaspoon pepper
½ teaspoon sugar
2 tablespoons butter
1 tablespoon flour
2 cups light cream, scalded
1 onion, peeled, whole

Shaker Pease Porridge

2 cups dried split peas
1 quart White Stock or stock from ham bone
2 onions, diced
2 carrots, diced
2 ribs celery, diced
1 turnip, diced
1 teaspoon salt
¼ teaspoon pepper

Bean Soup

2 cups dried navy beans or other dried beans
1 ham bone (not too well trimmed)
3 quarts water
2 cups diced celery
1 cup chopped onion
4 ripe tomatoes, cut into quarters
1 cup diced potatoes
Salt and pepper to tatse
1 tablespoon minced parsley

Shaker Fish Chowder

½ pound bacon, finely cut
2 onions, minced
4 pounds fresh fish fillets
2 cups thinly sliced raw potatoes, unpeeled
½ teaspoon salt
⅛ teaspoon white pepper
2 tablespoons flour
Boiling water to cover
2 cups light cream, scalded
1 cup cracker meal

Sauté bacon in a deep skillet or saucepan for 5 minutes. Add onion and sauté until transparent. Do not brown. Cut fish fillets into one-inch squares. Place a layer of fish, then layer of potatoes over sautéed onions. Sprinkle lightly with combined salt, pepper and flour. Repeat layering until fish is used. Add boiling water to cover and simmer 15 minutes. Add cream and cracker meal. Simmer 30 minutes longer. Fresh fishes such as red snapper, salmon or mullet make a tasty chowder, as do clams and scallops, or a combination of fish and shellfish. If desired, a cheesecloth herb bag may be cooked in the last 30 minutes with the chowder. Serve very hot. Makes 8 servings.

NORTH UNION THOUGHTS ON SOUP: "Combinations of herbs in soups are endless and make an interesting study."

"For broths, always start the soup with cold water; this will extract the greatest nourishment from the ingredients in your pot."

"Try a dash of nutmeg and pinch of sugar in most any soup."

"As an introduction to a good book whets one's interest in what is to follow, just so should a clear soup stimulate and enliven the most jaded appetite for a good dinner."

MAIN DISHES

The Elders' Workshop, Center Family,
North Union, Ohio

MAIN DISHES

May 4th, 1840. We arrived at North Union at six o'clock sharp and were heartily greeted in song by all members of the community. In a brief time we were summoned to supper when we had a meal of fresh fish of excellent quality. – Visitors to North Union.

Life was hard for the earliest Shakers, and food was not always plentiful in the pioneering years of the various societies. New Lebanon, the first Shaker society, was especially unfortunate; a famine was sweeping the area at the time of its founding, and it is said that some of the brethren were unable to run twenty rods because of weakness from lack of food.

Through hard work and scientific farming, however, the Shakers soon began to harvest bountiful crops at each of their communities, and their meals came to include generous portions of fresh fish, poultry, meat (except when vegetarianism prevailed), and products made from their own eggs and cheese. An article in *The Manifesto* said of the typical Shaker meal: "The table is completely furnished with food at intervals of four plates, and waiting sisters, who take monthly turns at this work, replenish the food-plates as fast as emptied.". As the following recipes suggest, after the early years the Shakers did not go hungry.

Tin cheese strainer from Alfred, Maine.

EGGS AND CHEESE

By 1850 it was found that the clay soil at North Union Shaker community was better adapted to raising herds than grain. In turn, the problem of marketing the milk of their large herds led to their making vast amounts of cheese. The Shakers became skilled cheesemakers, and soon their deep cellars and cold spring houses were richly stocked with ripening cheeses.

Eggs also were an important item of diet for the Shakers, and dozens went daily into the making of custards, cakes, muffins, noodles, omelets and other dishes for their large families. Moreover, the sisters saw to it that the wide eggbaskets were well filled when the Shaker peddler made his weekly rounds of nearby residents. Baskets of eggs, pats of neatly molded butter, crocks of pickles and preserves were the sisters' chief source of income for they, too, did their share in defraying the household expenses of the large establishments. This "egg money" was in turn spent for the ever-necessary lemons, nutmegs, pepper and salt and a few other items the self-sustaining communities could not raise.

Cheese Omelet

6 tablespoons soft butter
½ teaspoon prepared mustard
6 slices bread, cut in half diagonally
1 pound sharp cheddar, thinly sliced
4 eggs
2 cups half-and-half
½ teaspoon salt
¼ teaspoon pepper

Stir butter and mustard together. Spread on bread slices. Butter a 1½-quart baking dish and cover the bottom with bread triangles. Place cheese slices on bread; repeat with bread and cheese to make 2 layers. Beat eggs and half-and-half together and pour over bread and cheese layers. Season. Bake in an oven preheated to 350°F for 30 minutes. Serve very hot. Makes 4 to 5 servings.

Sister Mary, Enfield Shakers

Shaker Cheese Soufflé

2 tablespoons butter
2 tablespoons flour
1 cup half-and-half
½ teaspoon salt
¼ teaspoon pepper
Few grains cayenne
1 cup sharp cheddar, shredded
3 egg yolks
3 egg whites

In a saucepan, over low flame, melt butter, add flour and stir to blend well. Add half-and-half and stir until smooth. Season. Stir in cheese until blended, then slightly beaten yolks. Cool slightly. Beat egg whites until very stiff, but not dry, peaks are formed and fold into yolk mixture. Pour into a baking dish that has been buttered on the bottom only and set into a pan of hot water. Bake for 35 minutes in an oven that has been preheated to 325°F. Makes 3 to 4 servings.

Sister Abigail

Lentil Loaf

2 cups dried lentils
Cold water to cover
¼ pound mild cheddar
1 cup fresh bread crumbs
1 tablespoon grated onion
½ teaspoon fresh rosemary
1 teaspoon salt
⅛ teaspoon pepper
¼ cup melted butter

Place lentils in a saucepan. Cover with cold water and simmer over moderate heat until just tender, about 20 to 30 minutes. Do not overcook. Pass lentils and cheese through a food grinder. Add other ingredients and shape into loaf. Baste surface well with butter. Bake in an oven preheated to 350°F for 45 minutes. Baste often. Serves 4 to 6. Serve with Tasty Tomato Sauce or Mushroom Sauce (see Index).

South Union

Shaker Rarebit I

½ pound sharp cheddar cheese
2 cups light cream
½ teaspoon salt
⅛ teaspoon garlic powder
Few grains cayenne
8 rounds of toast, well buttered

Shred cheese and add to milk. Heat to the boiling point, stirring constantly until very smooth. Add seasoning and pour over rounds of toast. Serves 4.

Shaker Rarebit II

½ pound Swiss or Gruyère cheese
¾ cup cider or medium-dry white wine
⅛ teaspoon onion powder
½ teaspoon salt
Toasted bread slices

Slice cheese into thin slices. Lay in a flameproof baking dish and cover with cider. Let set 4 hours at room temperature. Place over low heat and stir until smooth. Pour over toast triangles, made from 6 to 8 slices of bread, and serve at once. Makes 4 servings.

Pleasant Hill, Kentucky

GLORIOUS CHEESE: During the Shaker ban on meat, cheese soufflés, noodles baked with cheese, rarebits and just sliced cheese took the place of meat at the great Shaker tables where fifty brethren ate on one side of the dining halls while fifty sisters occupied the tables on the other side.

MANY KINDS OF CHEESE: The Shakers made a large variety of cheese, ranging from cottage cheese to Yankee cheddars, as well as several herb-laden varieties which were remembered fondly by early settlers of Shaker Heights long after the Shakers had passed away.

Egg Croquettes

6 eggs, hard-cooked
2 tablespoons butter
2 tablespoons flour
¾ cup milk
½ teaspoon salt
¹⁄₁₆ teaspoon white pepper
Pinch of paprika
½ cup cracker crumbs
1 egg, beaten with 1 tablespoon
    water

Chop eggs finely. Make a roux by melting butter in the top of a double boiler and gradually blending in the flour. Add milk a little at a time, stirring well to form a smooth white sauce. Season with salt, pepper and paprika. Stir in chopped eggs and chill thoroughly. When cold, shape into 6 large or 12 small croquettes. Roll in cracker crumbs, then in beaten egg, and again in crumbs. Fry in deep fat (375°F) until golden brown. Serves six.

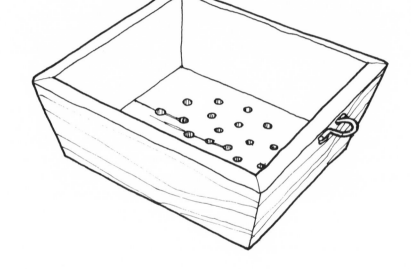

Wooden cheese box in old red, used to drain whey from curd.

Shaker Dropped (Poached) Eggs

6 eggs
2 cups water, boiling
½ teaspoon salt
1 teaspoon cider vinegar
6 rounds toast, buttered
⅛ teaspoon white pepper

Lay muffin rings in the bottom of a skillet and place over moderate heat. Add 2 cups boiling water to which salt and vinegar have been added. Break eggs into the rings (which keep eggs nice and round); the vinegar coagulates the whites. Just as soon as the whites set (about 3 to 4 minutes), remove egg and place on a round of buttered toast. Sprinkle with white pepper and serve immediately. Very appetizing.

　　NOTE: If muffin rings are unavailable, set well-buttered custard cups in the bottom of a deep saucepan. Place a few drops of vinegar and a dash of salt in each cup. Pour boiling water into each cup to fill and enough water in the pan to almost reach the top of each cup. Break eggs, one at a time, into each cup and remove to buttered toast rounds when whites have set (about 5 to 6 minutes.)

Beat egg whites until very stiff, but not dry. Spoon into a buttered baking dish. Make 4 wells or nests in whites and slip in the raw unbroken yolks. Mix bread crumbs with melted butter, salt and paprika and sprinkle over the surface. Bake 10 minutes, or until crumbs are nicely browned, in a preheated 350°F oven. Top with chives and serve hot. Serves four.

North Union

Add catsup or chili sauce and butter to hot rice and mix thoroughly. Reheat and place on a hot platter. Make six wells or nests in the rice and spoon the drained hot dropped eggs in them. Garnish with water cress. Serves six.

Cut the hard-cooked eggs in two, lengthwise; remove yolks. Pass the yolks through a sieve. Add next 6 ingredients. Mix thoroughly. Fill centers of egg halves and press them together. There will be a little of this mixture left over; add to whole egg and beat well. Roll whole stuffed eggs in this mixture and then in cracker crumbs. Fry in fat, heated to 375°F until golden brown. Serves 6.

SHAKER EGG HINTS: "Duck and goose eggs are very strong in flavor and should never be used in delicate cakes or custards. They are excellent, however, for well-seasoned scrambled eggs or in Spanish omelet."

"To soft cook an egg, three minutes is the allotted time."

"To hard cook an egg, eight to ten minutes is required. Roll eggs about gently while cooking so yolk does not settle to one side. Immerse hard-cooked egg into cold water as soon as cooked; this will keep the shell from sticking to white."

Shaker Shirred Eggs

4 egg whites
4 egg yolks (unbroken)
⅛ teaspoon salt
1/16 teaspoon paprika
2 tablespoons bread crumbs
2 tablespoons butter, melted
1 tablespoon chives, chopped

Spanish Eggs

1 cup converted rice, cooked
   according to package directions
1 cup tomato catsup or chili sauce
2 tablespoons butter
6 Dropped Eggs (see recipe)

Stuffed Eggs

6 eggs, hard cooked
2 teaspoons butter
1 tablespoon heavy cream
½ teaspoon salt
⅛ teaspoon pepper
1 teaspoon prepared mustard
½ teaspoon lemon juice
1 egg, uncooked
½ cup cracker crumbs

Eldress Clymena's Blue Flower Omelet

4 eggs
4 tablespoons milk or water
½ teaspoon salt
⅛ teaspoon pepper
1 tablespoon parsley, minced
1 teaspoon chives, minced
12 chive blossoms
2 tablespoons butter

This delicious omelet may be made when the chive blossoms are in full bloom. Pick over blossoms, then wash and drain thoroughly. Lightly beat eggs, just enough to blend whites and yolks well. Add milk or water, seasoning, minced parsley and chives. Melt butter in a heavy cast-iron skillet over fairly high heat, and pour in the egg mixture. When the edges of the omelet begin to set, reduce the heat to moderate. With a spatula, slash the uncooked parts to allow for even cooking. When the bottom is well browned, sprinkle the drained flowers over the omelet and fold in half, carefully. Serve immediately on a hot platter, alone, or with a delicately flavored cheese sauce. The blue blossoms add a delicious flavor and interest to the dish. Serves four.

North Union

Delicate Shaker Omelet

1 tablespoon flour
¼ cup cold milk
¾ cup warm milk
6 egg yolks
½ teaspoon salt
6 egg whites
2 tablespoons soft butter

Mix flour with cold milk and stir into warm milk. Beat in egg yolks and salt. Stir until smooth. Beat egg whites until stiff peaks are formed and fold them into the milk-yolks mixture. Pour into a buttered 2-quart baking dish and bake in a preheated slow (300°F) oven for 25 minutes. Serves 4.

Quaker Omelet

1½ tablespoons cornstarch
½ cup milk
3 eggs yolks
½ teaspoon salt
⅛ teaspoon pepper
¼ teaspoon ground marjoram
3 egg whites
1 tablespoon butter

Soften cornstarch in milk. Beat egg yolks until light and lemon colored. Beat in salt, pepper and marjoram. Stir in milk. Heat a cast-iron or heavy aluminum skillet over moderate heat. Beat egg whites until stiff peaks are formed. Fold into the yolk mixture. Pour into the hot skillet, in which the butter has been melted. Cover tightly and reduce heat to low. Cook slowly to brown gently without burning, about 7 minutes. Fold in half and slip onto a heated platter. Serve immediately. Serves 3.

Mary Whitcher's Shaker House-Keeper

Shaker Supper Omelet

½ cup hot, scalded milk
⅓ cup dry bread or cracker crumbs
1 teaspoon salt
¼ teaspoon pepper
3 eggs, beaten
1 tablespoon butter

Pour hot, scalded milk over crumbs. Let cool. Add salt and pepper and mix in well-beaten eggs. Heat cast-iron skillet over fairly high heat and add butter. Pour in egg mixture and reduce heat to moderate. Fry to a golden brown on the bottom. Be careful not to cook too fast, at too hot a temperature: the egg will toughen and the bottom will burn before the surface is set. When the omelet has set in all but the center, fold in half and slip onto a hot platter. Serve at once. Serves two.

North Union

Fresh Corn Soufflé

2 tablespoons sweet butter
2 tablespoons all-purpose flour
1 cup milk
3 egg yolks
½ teaspoon salt
⅛ teaspoon black pepper
2 cups fresh corn, grated from the cob
1 tablespoon sugar
3 egg whites

Make a white sauce by melting butter and stirring in flour with a wooden spoon, over low heat. Blend well. Stir in the milk until smooth. Stir in salt and pepper. Beat the egg yolks slightly and add to the white sauce. Mix thoroughly. Stir in corn and let cool slightly. Beat egg whites until soft peaks are formed. Add sugar and continue beating until stiff peaks are formed. Fold white sauce mixture into beaten egg whites. Pour mixture into a buttered 3-quart, straight-sided casserole or soufflé dish and bake 45 minutes in a preheated moderate (325°F) oven. Serve at once. Serves 6.

North Union

Tomato Custard

4 pounds ripe tomatoes
4 beaten eggs
1 cup milk
½ cup sugar
½ teaspoon salt
⅛ teaspoon nutmeg

Stew tomatoes in their own juices, without adding water. Pass through a sieve or food mill to form a strained puree. Cool and add to beaten eggs, milk, sugar and seasoning. Bake in 6 individual buttered custard cups for about 25 minutes in a preheated oven (325°F).

RESPECT YOUR SOUFFLE: "A soufflé must never be kept waiting!"—Sister Lisset.

MEAT

Although many Shakers practiced vegetarianism, and meat actually was banned for twelve years starting in the late 1830s, the practice of meat-eating varied over time and among Shaker families and individuals. Striving to be self-sufficient in the production of meat as in other things, the Shakers usually did their own butchering. Every fall on a frosty day in late November, the butcher knives were sharpened to a razor-edge, the mighty scalding cauldrons were gotten in readiness, the crude meat grinders and sausage guns were brought forth, and rows of huge earthen crocks, barrels and kegs were thoroughly cleansed and filled with brine stout enough to float an egg, awaiting the time when the surplus stock of the farm was converted into hams, corned brisket, sausage and tempting flitches of bacon.

Usually the slaughtering was taken care of by some of the brethren behind a distant barn screened from sight of the sisters and children. This autumn kill was an important part of rural life. If the pioneer Shaker wanted sustenance for his body, enabling him to perform his heavy labor and to go forth daily in his religious dance, corned-beef hash and pickled spareribs and sausages were highly desirable. Cooking fats, especially, were in constant demand among the frontiersmen. Nothing could be baked or fried without suitable fats.

While the Shaker brethren were dividing up the carcasses into suitable cuts, herbs and spices were weighed and measured by the sisters to give savor to sausage and tang to bologna. When saltpeter was available for curing meats, the older children ground it on the hominy block. Then hams and shoulders were laid in crisscross fashion in great barrels of sugar-cure awaiting the day when they would be suspended from the rafters of the smokehouse, where tiny fires of hickory chips or green corncobs were smoldering in iron pots. These smoldering embers imparted aroma and pungent flavor to the ripening viands.

Deep down in the coolest of their large cellars were barrels of corned beef and rows of crocks of herb-laden sausages and huge tubs of lard often delicately scented with leaf of bay or thyme. The Shakers, who abhorred waste, used every fragment of the kill: the feet of veal or pork were fashioned into dainty jelly for gelatin dishes for the aged and infirm; the heads were boiled and converted into appetitizing loaves of scrapple or head-cheese, so tasty for breakfast on frosty mornings. The tripe, kidneys and liver went into aromatic stews and succulent dinner dishes, while the hearts, jowls, sweetbreads and brains were disguised into toothsome pressed meats encased in jelly. Even the bladder was blown up and given to the children as a new ball, while the curly pigtail was salvaged and hung beside the Shaker brethren's workbench to grease the saws.

For several days following the sad event, the great Shaker kitchens thrice daily poured forth the pungent aroma of roasts, steaks and chops being prepared with rosemary, thyme and summer savory. In a day when mechanical refrigeration was unknown, these fresh meats had to be eaten almost immediately. These feasts of fresh meats were followed by months of salted, dried and smoked meats. Chickens, rabbits, an occasional wild turkey or a joint of venison at times brought relief from the monotonous salt-meat diet.

Beef Stew with Herbs

Mix flour, salt and pepper. Heat oil to 375°F in a Dutch oven with a cover. Dredge cubes of meat in seasoned flour and brown well in the hot oil. Add onion and sauté with meat for 10 minutes. Add liquids, cover tightly and simmer slowly for about 2 hours. Add a few drops of liquid occasionally, if needed. During the last half hour add remaining ingredients and check seasoning. Simmer until vegetables are tender (15 to 20 minutes). Serves 4.

1 tablespoon flour
1 teaspoon salt
¼ teaspoon pepper
¼ cup oil
1 pound boneless beef, cut into 1½ inch cubes
1 large onion, sliced
½ cup cider or dry white wine
½ cup water or stock
¼ cup marjoram, minced
½ teaspoon thyme, minced
2 carrots, diced
2 turnips, diced
6 celery leaves

Corned Beef and Cabbage

Soak beef in cold water for an hour. Drain and cover with fresh cold water and bring to a boil. Skim surface well. Let simmer very gently for 3 to 4 hours. Thirty minutes before meat is done, remove some of the cooking liquid. In a separate pot, simmer the peeled potatoes, turnips, carrots and onions for 15 minutes. Add the cabbage and cook 15 minutes longer. Lift the brisket onto a large, well-heated platter and surround with the cooked vegetables. Serve with fresh horseradish or spicy mustard. Serves six.

4 pounds corned beef brisket
6 medium potatoes
6 medium turnips
6 medium carrots
6 medium onions
1 small cabbage, cut into 6 wedges

Shaker Beef Stew

4 pounds beef for stew
Salt and pepper
Flour for dredging
3 tablespoons butter
2 quarts boiling water
2 pounds small potatoes, partially
    peeled
5 medium-size onions, peeled
8 medium carrots, scraped
8 medium turnips, peeled and halved
3 ribs celery, cut into 6-inch lengths

Cut beef into 1-inch cubes. Mix together salt, pepper and flour. Dredge meat in this mixture. Melt butter in a Dutch oven over fairly high heat and brown meat cubes quickly. Add boiling water, cover and simmer gently for 1½ hours. Add potatoes, onions, carrots, turnips and celery. Simmer for another 30 minutes. Use the dumpling mixture and drop into stew by spoonfuls (see Index for Dumplings). Cover tightly and cook 12 minutes more. Serves 6 to 8.

Mary Whitcher's Shaker House-Keeper

Shaker Flank Steak

3 pounds flank steak or chuck
    shoulder steak
2 tablespoons flour
2 tablespoons butter
2 onions, chopped
1 teaspoon salt
⅛ teaspoon pepper
Juice of ½ lemon
2 tablespoons celery, minced
2 tablespoons carrot, minced
2 tablespoons green pepper, minced
¼ cup tomato catsup
2 cups boiling water or stock

A flank steak has long fibers, so cut or score the surface on a diagonal with a sharp knife. Dredge in flour. Melt butter in a heat-proof dutch oven over high heat and brown surface of the meat quickly. Add remaining ingredients in order, cover, and cook in a preheated oven (300°F) for about 2½ to 3 hours, or until meat is tender. Its own rich gravy will be formed during cooking. Serve with noodles, rice, dumplings, or parslied potatoes. Serves six.

The Shakers used this recipe when flank steak (London Broil) was very inexpensive, and considered a "cheap" cut of meat. Any less tender cut of meat, about inch thick (such as boneless chuck steak) may be used.

Amelia's Shaker Recipes

SHAKER SPICED SALT: Spiced salt should always be kept on hand. It is easily made by mixing 1½ teaspoons each of powdered thyme, bay leaf, black pepper and nutmeg with ¼ teaspoon cayenne pepper and marjoram to which you add 3 teaspoons powdered cloves. Sift these together and put in a tightly closed canister. To this add 3 tablespoons salt. Keep canister well closed. This is an outstanding seasoning for soups, dressings and meat.

NORTH UNION GRAVY HINTS: "Never throw away the water in which vegetables have been cooked. Always use as little water in cooking vegetables as posssible. This pot-liquor or vegetable water contains nourishment and flavor and should be used in making gravys, sauces and stews."

"Rice and barley water are also good binders for sauces and stews."

In a bowl, blend together all ingredients except crumbs and cheese. Place mixture in a buttered baking dish and sprinkle surface with crumbs and cheese, or dot with butter. Place in an oven preheated to 350°F and cook until well browned. Serves four.

VARIATIONS:

1. Add 3 eggs, slightly beaten, to meat and vegetable mixture. Form into balls or patties, dredge in bread crumbs and fry until golden brown, OR
2. Over moderate heat, place meat and vegetable mixture into a greased, preheated skillet. Fry until underside is brown. Invert onto a platter and slip back into skillet to brown the other side.
3. Any cooked meat or poultry may be substituted for beef in the recipe.

Place meat in a baking pan. Score surface slightly by cutting shallow slice on a diagonal, across the leg at three-inch intervals. Melt butter and dip in rosemary stalks. Brush surface of roast with buttered stalks to coat thoroughly. If fresh rosemary is not available, mix crushed, dried leaves with butter and rub onto the meat. Dredge in flour mixed with salt and pepper. Roast in a preheated slow oven (250°F) for 3 hours, basting frequently with pan juices. Serve with mashed parsnips, turnips, rutabaga, or Jerusalem artichokes. Serves 8 to 10.

Amelia's Shaker Recipes

If a country cured ham is used, scrub ham thoroughly and soak overnight in cold water. Drain water and refill with cold water to cover. Bring to a rapid boil. Reduce heat and simmer for about 3 hours. Let ham cool in the cooking liquid. If the ham has been precooked, it will not need cooking. Remove rind and trim fat. Place in a roasting pan, on a rack in a preheated 450°F oven to sear the surface. Stud with cloves.

Combine boiling water, cider, brown sugar and onions and boil 10 minutes. Strain and pour over ham. Reduce oven temperature to 350°F and bake 1 hour, basting every 15 minutes. In a skillet, over low heat, brown the flour. Add the butter to form a roux. Strain liquid from ham, add lemon juice and add to the brown roux, stirring constantly until smooth. Serve this as a sauce with the ham. Serves 12 to 16.

Sister Content's Hash

2 cups cold cooked beef, minced
1 cup cold cooked potatoes, diced
½ cup onion, chopped
⅓ cup green pepper, chopped
1 cup mushroom gravy
Salt and pepper
1 tablespoon butter
1/16 teaspoon paprika
¼ cup bread crumbs
1½ teaspoons grated cheese
OR 1½ teaspoons butter

Shaker Roast Leg of Lamb

6-to-7 pound leg of lamb, dressed
    and trimmed
2 tablespoons butter
8 stalks fresh rosemary
OR ½ teaspoon dried leaves
1 tablespoon flour
½ teaspoon salt
⅛ teaspoon pepper

Ham Baked in Cider

10 to 12 pound ham, bone in
Cold water to cover
24 whole cloves
1 cup boiling water
1 quart Cider Concentrate
2 tablespoons brown sugar
2 small onions, chopped
1½ tablespoons flour
1 tablespoon butter
2 tablespoons lemon juice

Roast of Pork

5 or 6 pound boneless pork roast
Juice of ½ lemon
1 teaspoon flour
1 teaspoon salt
½ teaspoon powdered onion
¹⁄₁₆ teaspoon pepper
10 small unpeeled potatoes
5 carrots, cut into 2-inch lengths

Rub lemon juice onto the roast. Mix flour and seasonings and dredge roast. Place on a rack in a shallow pan and roast in a preheated oven (325°F) for about 2½ hours or until a thermometer inserted to a depth of 2 inches reaches 180°F. When temperature reaches 160°F, or the last half hour of cooking, surround roast with potatoes and carrots. Serves 8 to 10.

North Union

Shaker Scrapple

1½ pounds raw, lean pork
1 pound pork fat
3 quarts of broth from cooked meat
1½ teaspoon salt
⅛ teaspoon sage
⅛ teaspoon marjoram
½ teaspoon black pepper
2 cups white cornmeal
2 cups whole wheat flour

Cut raw pork and fat into large chunks. Simmer in 4 quarts of water until tender, about 1½ to 2 hours. Skim off melted fat and reserve. Drain and reserve 3 quarts of broth. Remove meat and discard fat. Chop meat fine and measure about 2 generous cups. Bring reserved broth to a boil and add herbs and seasonings. Mix cornmeal and flour and stir into boiling mixture. Stir in chopped meat.

Cook slowly in a Dutch oven or other heavy pot for 30 minutes, stirring frequently. Pour into loaf or tube pans to desired thickness (smaller loaves keep better). Ladle a small amount of fat on top of each loaf to help preserve the scrapple. If desired, melted bacon fat may be used instead of the pork fat. Chill thoroughly. To serve, slice ½ inch thick, dredge slices in flour, and fry in ½ inch hot bacon fat until well browned on both sides.

North Union

Jellied Veal

4 veal shanks, split
2 quarts water
⅛ teaspoon pepper
1 teaspoon salt
1 bay leaf
⅛ teaspoon mace
2 stalks celery, minced
8 sprigs parsley, minced
1 cooked carrot, minced
1 tablespoon minced green pepper
1 teaspoon fresh chervil, cut

Slowly simmer the shanks in water with salt, pepper and mace, until tender, about 3 hours. Remove shanks, separate the meat from bones, and shred. Cool stock to below 140°F. Stir in 3 eggs, crushed, with shells. Bring to a boil and hold there for 5 minutes. Strain through several layers of cheesecloth to clarify. Cool until stock has become thick and syrupy. Fold in meat, vegetables and remaining herbs and pour into a 2-quart mold or loaf pan. Chill until firm. To serve, slice and serve on a bed of lettuce with a piquant dressing.

Canterbury

Sister Lettie's Veal Loaf

3 eggs
1 cup light cream or half-and-half
⅔ cup cracker meal
3 pounds ground veal
½ pound ground pork or sausage
2 teaspoons salt
1 teaspoon sage
1 medium onion, finely minced
¼ teaspoon pepper
1 teaspoon celery seed
4 slices bacon
3 tablespoons flour
1 cup milk or vegetable liquor

Beat eggs and cream together. Stir in all remaining ingredients except bacon, flour and milk or vegetable liquor. Mix thoroughly. Shape into a long, roll-shaped loaf. Place in a greased roasting pan and lay strips of bacon over the surface to allow for self-basting. Bake for 1½ to 2 hours, in an oven preheated to 300°F, or until a meat thermometer inserted at the center registers 180°F. Remove to heated platter and reserve drippings. Pour two tablespoons drippings from the roasting pan into an iron skillet, heated over moderate heat. Stir in the flour and cook to brown. Gradually add the milk or vegetable liquor, stirring constantly to avoid lumping. Serves 8 to 10.

Baked Liver with Onions

1 Bermuda onion, sliced
2 tablespoons butter
¼ cup hot water
6 slices veal or lamb liver
4 tablespoons flour
Salt and pepper
1 bay leaf
8 sprigs parsley
2 sprigs thyme

Place slices of onion in a well-buttered 2-quart casserole. Melt butter in hot water and pour over onion. Remove tubes and membrane from liver and dredge in flour seasoned with salt and pepper. Arrange liver slices over onions, add herbs and dot with butter. Bake covered, in a preheated oven (350°F), for 30 minutes. Uncover, remove herbs, and return to oven to brown liver. Herbs may be placed in a cheesecloth herb bag or tied together with thread to make removal easier.

SCRAPPLE TIME: Scrapple had a definite season. It started with the first fall frost and lasted until the return of warm weather the following spring. Because of the fat content of the pork, scrapple did not keep in warm weather. Scrapple was an excellent way of using up pork scraps when butchering, which may explain its name. A Pennsylvania Dutch dish, scrapple may have come into the Shaker cookery collection through the small and shortlived Philadelphia Shaker society.

Baked Beef Tongue

1 fresh beef tongue, about 4 pounds
Water to cover
1 teaspoon salt
2 cups tomatoes, diced
1 small onion, diced
3 ribs celery, minced
½ teaspoon salt
1/16 teaspoon pepper

Simmer tongue in salted water until tender, 2 to 2½ hours. Reserve ½ cup stock. When cool enough, remove skin from tongue and trim bones, fat and gristle. Place into a large covered casserole with tomatoes, onion, celery, salt and pepper. Add 2 tablespoons flour to reserved, cooled stock and pour into casserole. Bake in a preheated moderate (375°F) oven for 45 minutes. Makes about 8 servings.

The Manifesto

Kidney and Steak Pie

4 veal kidneys
Water to cover
1 recipe biscuit or pastry dough
½ pound beef sirloin, diced
1 cup raw potatoes, sliced
1 small onion, sliced
2 hard cooked eggs, sliced
Salt and pepper

Remove all fiber and excess fat from kidneys. Refrigerate overnight in water. Simmer slowly in the same water until tender. Remove kidneys and reserve stock. Thinly slice kidneys. Line a buttered 1½- to 2-quart casserole with a thin layer of rolled dough. Arrange kidneys, beef, potatoes, onion and eggs on dough. Repeat until all ingredients are used. Pour reserved stock over all and sprinkle with seasoning. Top with a thinly rolled dough crust and crimp edges to seal. Allow a steam-vent hole in the top (see suggestions for pastry). Bake in a preheated hot (450°F) oven 15 minutes to brown, then at 350°F for 40 minutes. Serves 6.

Mary Whitcher's Shaker House-Keeper

Broiled Sweetbreads

2 pairs sweetbreads
4 cups cold water
½ teaspoon salt
Juice of ½ lemon
2 tablespoons melted butter
⅛ teaspoon nutmeg

Lay sweetbreads in cold water for an hour, changing water several times. Then cover with cold water to which salt and lemon juice have been added. Simmer gently for 15 minutes. Immediately plunge sweetbreads into cold water to cool quickly. Remove all fat and membrane. Place sweetbreads on a platter and place another platter on top. Weight the top platter to flatten meat and let remain in the refrigerator for at least one hour. Brush with butter and sprinkle with nutmeg. Broil at 3 inches from the source of heat for about 5 minutes. Turn, brush surface with butter and finish for about 3 minutes. Makes 4 to 6 servings.

NUTRITIOUS DELICACIES: "Only veal, lamb or mutton sweetbreads are used in cookery. They are a great delicacy and should be enjoyed more often. All the viscera, heart, kidneys, liver, tripe and sweetbreads are highly nutritious and can be made into very inviting dishes with a little thought and care."— Sister Lottie.

Shaker Sweetbreads

1 pair sweetbreads
Water to cover
½ teaspoon salt
1 teaspoon lemon juice
2 tablespoons butter
2 tablespoons flour
1 tablespoon lemon juice
½ teaspoon salt
1/16 teaspoon pepper
2 egg yolks
1 tablespoon minced parsley
6 toast rounds or rusk

Parcook sweetbreads in 3 to 4 cups water to which salt and lemon juice have been added. Drain, reserving broth. Carefully trim any fat and all membrane. Cut into half-inch squares. Melt butter and blend in flour to form a roux. Add 2 cups of the broth, lemon juice, salt and pepper. Cook gently to form a velouté (white sauce). Beat egg yolks until frothy and pour in a little of the hot velouté. Beat the yolk mixture into the remaining sauce, add sweetbreads, and heat to 160°F, until sauce thickens. Serve on rounds or points of toast, in a pastry shell, or over rice; sprinkle with parsley. Serve immediately with an accompaniment of green peas. Makes 4 servings.

Tripe with Mustard Sauce

1 pound honeycomb tripe,
  defrosted
½ cup flour
¼ teaspoon salt
1/16 teaspoon pepper
1/16 teaspoon paprika
1/16 teaspoon garlic powder
2 eggs
¾ cup bread crumbs
1 tablespoon grated parmesan cheese
1 tablespoon finely chopped
  parsley
¼ cut butter

Tripe is available parcooked, frozen or thawed, in most supermarkets. Select only "honeycomb tripe." It is that which is described by Sister Lisset, and is of excellent quality.

Simmer defrosted tripe in water, until tender. Cut into strips, 1 inch by 3 inches. Dip the pieces in flour, seasoned with salt, pepper, paprika and garlic powder. Dip in egg, then in bread crumbs seasoned with grated parmesan cheese and finely chopped parsley. Fry in butter until golden brown. Serve with Mustard Sauce (see Index) to accompany.

MOTHER ANN'S ECONOMY WITH FOOD: Mother Ann Lee, founder of the Shaker church, taught her followers not to waste food. "I have seen her walk from end to end of the table, picking the bones after us, and eating the broken bits of bread which the multitude had left," a contemporary wrote. "Sometimes the Elders, or some others, would urge her to have something better; but she would reply, 'It is good enough for me, for it is the blessing of God, and must not be lost. You must be prudent, and saving of every good thing which God blesses you with, so that you may have wherewith to give to them that stand in need.'"

POULTRY

Chicken Gelatin

2 tablespoons gelatin
¼ cup cold water
2 cups chicken stock
½ teaspoon salt
⅛ teaspoon paprika
3 hard-cooked eggs
1 tablespoon minced parsley
3 cups cooked, sliced chicken

Sprinkle gelatin into cold water and let stand to soften for 5 minutes. Heat chicken stock to boiling and disperse softened gelatin in it. Add salt and paprika. Pour ½ cup gelatin mixture into a 1-quart mold. Chill until firm. Slice eggs, arrange on gelatin, and sprinkle with minced parsley. Add about ¼ cup liquid gelatin mixture to set eggs and parsley. Chill until firm. Arrange chicken slices on surface of firm gelatine and add about ½ cup liquid gelatin mixture. Chill until firm. Pour remaining gelatin mixture into mold and chill until firm. Makes 6 servings.

   To unmold the gelatin, run the tip of a sharp, pointed knife around edge of the mold, into the jelly. Dip mold quickly into lukewarm water, to the depth of the jelly in the mold. Place an inverted plate on the open end of the mold and invert quickly. Sometimes one or two firm shakes will be necessary to allow the jelly to drop from the mold onto the plate.

Sister Lisset

Sister Clymena's Chicken Pie

2 chickens, 3 pounds each
3 cups chicken stock
3 eggs
2 cups heavy cream
1 small onion, minced
4 sprigs parsley, minced
1 teaspoon dried chervil
Salt and pepper to taste
1½ recipe Biscuits (see Index)
1 egg
2 tablespoons milk or cream

Disjoint chickens and simmer, well covered, in chicken stock for 30 minutes. Remove chicken from pan and take meat from carcass in large pieces. Beat together eggs, 1½ cups stock, all of the cream, herbs and seasoning. Butter a 3-quart baking dish well and line bottom and sides with rolled biscuit dough. Fill with chicken mixture. Cover with remaining dough and place a vent hole in the center to allow steam to escape. Fashion a foil or waxed paper cone and cut the point off. Place in the vent to allow juices to expand without running off. Make an egg wash by beating egg with milk. Brush onto the surface crust. Bake for 30 minutes in an oven preheated to 425°F. Serve immediately with a crisp green salad. Makes 4 to 6 servings.

North Union

ADVICE FOR CHICKEN BREEDERS: According to a Shaker farm journal found in the Western Reserve Historical Society, "The average farmer is careless about his feathered flocks. All young crowers should be gotten ready for the pot, sold or exchanged for several roosters of some good outside flock in order to keep your stock from inbreeding."

Chicken Pot Pie

1 recipe biscuit or pastry dough
4 cups cooked chicken meat
6 small raw potatoes
2 cups uncooked green peas
4 sprigs fresh marjoram, minced
4 sprigs parsley, minced
3 cups light cream
2 eggs, beaten

Roll out dough to ¼-inch thickness and line only the sides of a 3-quart casserole with it. Peel potatoes and slice thinly. Place a layer of chicken meat in the bottom and cover with a layer of potatoes. Sprinkle with peas, salt and pepper. Lay a few strips of dough across the surface and sprinkle with herbs. Repeat layers of chicken, potatoes, peas and dough, until casserole is ¾ filled. Add cream to eggs and pour into casserole over the layers. Top with a thinly rolled dough crust and crimp edges to seal. Allow a steam vent hole in the top (see suggestions for preparing pastry). Bake in a preheated moderate (350°F) oven for 45 minutes. Makes 6 servings.

Amelia's Shaker Recipes

Black walnut chest-on-chest, 71" tall. Made at North Union in the mid nineteenth century, it was used in the dining room of the Center Family for holding dishes. It is put together entirely with wooden pegs.

Shaker Fried Chicken

2 frying chickens, 2½ lbs. each
6 tablespoons butter, melted
1 tablespoon parsley, minced
¼ teaspoon dried marjoram
2 tablespoons flour
Salt and pepper
2 tablespoons butter
4 tablespoons bacon drippings or lard
1 cup light cream

Wash and dry chickens. Cut them into 16 pieces. Mix herbs with melted butter and coat chicken thoroughly. Let stand at room temperature for one hour. Mix salt and pepper with flour and dredge chicken in this to coat thoroughly. In a Dutch oven, over moderate heat, melt butter and bacon drippings. Add coated chicken and cook to brown pieces well. Pour cream over and let simmer, covered, for 20 minutes. Garnish with watercress and serve with a green salad. Serves six to eight.

Eldress Clymena Miner

Roast Game Birds

1 young guinea hen
OR 3 squab
OR 2 Cornish hens
2 cups fresh bread, crumbled
1 cup celery leaves, minced
1 teaspoon salt
3 tablespoons butter, melted
Juice of ½ lemon
½ cup hot water
2 egg yolks
1 cup cream
Salt and pepper

Mix bread, celery, salt and butter, and stuff bird(s) with mixture. Rub each bird with part of lemon juice and place in roaster. Baste with water and remainder of lemon juice. Cover tightly and roast in a moderately low (325°F) oven about 1 hour. Pour off juice and beat in egg yolks, cream, salt and pepper. Pour over bird and bake 30 minutes longer, uncovered. Serves 3 to 4.

North Union

STRUTTING BIRDS: The Shakers prided themselves on their thoroughbred herds; they also raised fine poultry—some famous as egg producers, while others were raised because they made succulent, meaty pies, stews and broths. At North Union not only guinea fowls were raised, but pea-fowls also strutted about. There is no explanation given for raising these vain, haughty creatures except that they ornamented the enclosed garden about the Office of the Ministry or guest house. However, because of the commotion the birds cause when disturbed, it's possible they were employed as "security guards." The eggs of the guinea fowls were believed to be of a special fine flavor when hard cooked and the flesh of the noisy, speckled little bird is a great delicacy.

Melt butter in heavy skillet and sauté onion in it until onion is transparent, but not brown. Add bread pieces, seasonings, herbs and chestnuts or potato. Mix thoroughly to combine well. Add half of the butter to water or stock, and when melted, add mixture to dressing and mix well to combine. Stuff chicken; skewer and truss to hold in dressing. Rub the skin well with the remaining soft butter and dust with salt.

Eldress Clymena

Wash bird inside and out. Melt butter in hot water or stock. Add bread, chestnuts, seasonings and herbs. Stuff neck and body cavities and sew or skewer-truss and lace bird so dressing does not run out. Spread with soft butter, sprinkle with cornmeal, and dust with salt and pepper. Bake in a preheated oven (325°F) for approximately 4 to 5 hours or until a thermometer placed in the thickest muscle of one thigh reaches 190°F. Baste often with pan juices. Serve with cranberry sauce, creamed turnips or onions, whipped squash and steamed dumplings; and plenty of turkey gravy. Serves 8 to 10.

The modern variation for roasting a turkey is to place it on a rack, breast down, in a shallow pan. Cover surface of the bird with bacon strips. When thermometer reaches 175°F, turn bird over to brown the breast.

South Union

Shaker Stuffing for Chicken

3 tablespoons butter
2 medium onions, minced
3 cups dried bread bits and pieces
½ cup celery leaves, chopped
1 tablespoon summer savory, chopped
1 teaspoon basil, cut fine
1 teaspoon thyme, crumbled
1 teaspoon salt
⅛ teaspoon pepper
10 chestnuts, blanched and quartered
OR 1 sweet potato, diced
½ cup hot water or stock
6 tablespoons soft butter
⅛ teaspoon salt

Roast (Wild) Turkey

Dressed turkey, 12 to 14 pounds
1 cup butter
1 cup hot water or stock
2 loaves stale white bread, broken into pieces
2 cups chestnuts, cooked and chopped
OR 2 cups diced parcooked sweet potatoes
Salt and pepper to taste
1 teaspoon thyme, minced
1 teaspoon ground marjoram

FISH AND SHELLFISH

In May, 1837, a Shaker elder visiting North Union wrote in his travel journal how the brethren brought the evening's dinner home to the Valley of God's Pleasure, and how the sisters prepared it:

"May 5th...and another real summer day! Last evening a number of the Brethren went fishing in Lake Erie. Toward noon today they brought home their catch—except the small ones which they always cast into their mill-pond on the way home. They had enough fish for all three Families [200 persons]; there were several muskies, a fine haul of white fish, a number of pike along with a lot of catfish and other kinds. They are all splendid eating. This evening we had a good supper of boiled catfish with herb-sauce, fried potatoes, boiled greens, pickled peppers, hot bread and lemon pie and tea....May 8th. We have had fresh fish every day since we arrived and sometimes twice; they know we like it!"

Shaker Baked Fish

2-to-3 pound fish, whole
6 unsalted soda crackers, crushed
1 teaspoon salt
1 tablespoon parsley, minced
1 tablespoon thyme, minced
1 tablespoon butter
Fish broth to moisten
4 strips bacon
Salt and cornmeal for dredging

If dried herbs are used, reduce the amount stated for the fresh to 1½ teaspoons. Scrape fish well to remove scales. Clean, dress, remove head and tail, and wash thoroughly. Use head and tail to make broth. Combine crackers, salt, herbs, butter and warm fish broth to moisten. Stuff the fish and fasten with skewers or toothpicks and "lace" with a string to fasten. Cut a few shallow diagonal slashes across the fish at 1- or 2-inch intervals. Dredge with cornmeal and salt. Lay strips of bacon on slashes and place fish in a buttered baking dish. Bake in a preheated slow oven (300°F) for approximately 1 hour. Remove to a hot platter and surround with Tomato Sauce (see Index). Garnish with lemon wedges and minced parsley or chives. Serves four to six.

Mary Whitcher's Shaker House-Keeper

SHAKER HINTS FOR FISH: "Catfish is extremely rich and fat, therefore boiling with vegetables is the best method of cooking it; the vegetables absorb some of the fatty flavor. It is a very interesting dish when thus prepared."

"Chervil, tarragon and mushrooms combined with lemon juice all make excellent flavorings for sauces served with fish."

TAKE CARE WITH FISH: "Few foods take as careful cooking as fish, for it must be thoroughly done but is very unappetizing if overdone."—Eldress Clymena.

Boiled Catfish

1 catfish, about 4 pounds
18-inch length of cheesecloth
2 tablespoons white vinegar
Water to cover
1 medium turnip, diced
1 medium carrot, diced
1 rib celery
5 medium parsnips, diced
1 medium onion, diced
4 sprigs parsley
Salt and pepper to taste
¼ teaspoon dried tarragon

Remove head and tail; clean, skin and wash fish. Be sure fish is VERY FRESH. Place fish into a poacher or long, covered roasting pan, and cover with water. Add vinegar. Let stand 20 minutes. Remove fish. Add diced vegetables and herbs and seasonings and place over moderate heat to simmer. Wrap prepared fish in cheesecloth, tie securely and place into simmering water. Cover and simmer 40 to 45 minutes. Remove cheesecloth carefully and place fish on a warm platter. Reserve fish stock for use in making a sauce. Serve very hot with Horseradish Sauce (see Index). Serves 6 to 8.

North Union

Shaker Codfish Cakes

2 cups codfish, shredded
1 cups raw potatoes, diced
1 tablespoon butter
1 small onion, grated
1 egg, beaten
Few grains of pepper
Nutmeg for dusting

Cook the raw, unsoaked, salted codfish in boiling water with raw potato until potato is done. Drain well and discard liquid. Add butter, onion, egg, and spices and mash well, until no lumps remain. Heat ½ inch oil in a cast-iron skillet to 375°F. Drop in fish mixture by tablespoonfuls and fry to a golden brown on each side. Do not soak the fish before boiling, and avoid too much handling of fish mixture. Serve with crisp slices of bacon and Rich Fish Sauce (see Index). Serves 6. Fishcakes may be dredged in bread or cracker crumbs or cornmeal before frying for an interesting variation.

Sister Lisset, North Union

A SHAKER PICNIC: A visting elder told how members of the North Union Ministry took their visitor to see the sights at the Lake Erie shore, and then laid out a roadside picnic: "Eldress Vincy and Sister Lucy served up a fine dinner for us, 'in real Ohio fashion,' they claimed. In no time over a little fire they boiled potatoes, cooked fresh asparagus from their own garden and made 'Shaker Fish and Eggs' with even a kettle of tea in the bargain! It being almost three o'clock when our dinner was served we were quite hungry and ate every morsel with great relish. We reached home about six after a most comfortable and pleasant day."

Shaker Fish and Eggs

2 cups light cream
  or half-and-half
1 tablespoon butter
¼ teaspoon salt
⅛ teaspoon pepper
¼ teaspoon dried rosemary
¼ cup green onions, chopped
3 medium-size boiled potatoes
1 cup cooked codfish, flaked
6 hard-cooked eggs

Flaked, cooked salt or fresh cod may be used for this dish. Heat cream with butter and seasonings to the simmering point. In a 2-quart, buttered baking dish place a layer of sliced, boiled potatoes. Sprinkle with finely shredded codfish and layer with sliced hard-cooked eggs. Reserve one egg for garnish. Repeat layering as necessary. Cover with heated cream and cook in a pre-heated oven (350°F) for 20 minutes. Garnish top with minced hard cooked eggs. Serves six.

Mary Whitcher's Shaker House-Keeper

Shaker Fish Balls

2 cups cooked fish, boned, skinned
  and flaked
4 cups cooked, or leftover cooked
  potatoes
1 small onion, grated
2 egg yolks, beaten
1 tablespoon parsley, minced
1/16 teaspoon nutmeg
Salt and pepper to taste
6 slices bacon, crisp

Place fish into a chopping bowl, on a chopping board, or in a food proces-sor. Be sure fish is boneless. Add potatoes to fish and chop together, or process until very fine. Add remaining ingredients and form into balls the size of a small egg. Keep hands floured when forming balls, to keep mixture from sticking. Heat about 3 inches of oil to 375°F and drop in balls, one at a time. Fry until golden brown. Slices of crisp bacon and White Sauce, Rich Fish Sauce, or Tomato Sauce (see Index) may be served with these croquettes. Serves six.

Sister Lisset, North Union

Oyster Pie

Rich pastry for 2 large crusts
2 tablespoons flour
⅛ teaspoon dried thyme
1 teaspoon salt
⅛ teaspoon pepper
1 quart shucked oysters
2½ tablespoons butter
1 egg
¼ cup milk or light cream
3 tablespoons chopped chives

Line a deep pie dish (or a 1½-quart straight-sided casserole) with pastry. Combine flour and seasonings and sprinkle the surface of the pastry with a third of the flour mixture. Drain oysters, reserving liquid. Place a layer of oysters in the dish, sprinkle with another third of the flour mixture and dot the surface with half of the butter. Repeat layering once more; pour on reserved oyster liquid, and sprinkle with chopped chives. Cover with top crust, taking care to place a vent hole in the center. Bake in a preheated 400°F oven for 7 minutes to set crust. Roll out remaining scraps of dough and cut into tiny fish or other shapes. Remove pie from oven and brush surface with a mixture of the egg and milk. Place cut shapes on top and brush again. Reduce heat to 350°F and continue cooking 25 minutes longer, until crust is nicely browned and contents of pie are bubbling.

Oyster Stew

4 tablespoons butter
1 pint shucked oysters
2 cups half-and-half or light cream
½ teaspoon salt
⅛ teaspoon pepper
1 tablespoon parsley, minced
1 teaspoon celery leaves, minced

In the top part of a double boiler, over low direct heat, melt butter, but do not brown. Drain oysters, reserving liquid, and pour into butter. Heat to the boiling point. Set the top part of the double boiler into the bottom part, containing hot water, over low heat. Pour in cream and reserved liquid. Add seasonings. When the oysters rise to the top, remove from heat. Pour into a deep, heated soup server or tureen and sprinkle surface with celery and parsley. Serve very hot. Serves two or three.

Union Village

Creamed Oysters

½ medium onion, thinly sliced
1/16 teaspoon mace
2 cups light or medium cream
1 tablespoon flour
1 tablespoon butter
½ teaspoon salt
⅛ teaspoon pepper
1 quart shucked oysters
8 to 10 toast rounds

In a saucepan, place onion and mace into cream and heat to simmering. Do not boil. Melt butter in another saucepan, over low heat, and stir in flour to form a roux. Gradually add the heated cream, stirring constantly until thickened. Strain and reserve liquid. Replace strained sauce to a saucepan, over low heat and add oysters. Heat only to the simmering point. Pour immediately over hot buttered toast rounds and serve immediately, with a crisp salad or slaw. Serves four or five.

Fried Oysters

1 quart shucked oysters
1 cup flour
Salt and pepper to taste
1/16 teaspoon ground thyme
1 cup cornmeal
2 eggs, beaten with 3 tablespoons water

Drain oysters and reserve liquid. Pat dry between paper towels. Combine flour with seasonings and dredge oysters in this combination, then in the egg mixture, and then in the cornmeal, to coat thoroughly. Drop into oil that has been heated to 375°F. Fry until golden brown. Drain on absorbent paper and remove to hot platter. Mix reserved oyster liquid with any remaining egg and cornmeal. Drop mixture by spoonfuls into hot oil and fry to a golden brown. Serve along with the oysters for added interest. Serves four to six.

THE OYSTER VOGUE: The popularity of oysters is said to have reached its peak around 1840, and the Shakers appear to have shared in America's enthusiasm for the mollusk. "The Oyster Express"—a vehicle loaded with live oysters covered with straw kept wet with salt water—traveled as far inland as Cincinnati to serve customers at the myriad oyster bars and other establishments catering to the demand.

Salmon Loaf

2 cups salmon, cooked or canned
1½ cups bread crumbs
OR 2 cups cooked white or brown
rice
½ cup milk or half-and-half
2 eggs, beaten
1½ tablespoons parsley, minced
1 tablespoon melted butter
1 teaspoon salt
1 teaspoon lemon juice

Flake salmon and stir in remaining ingredients. Mold mixture into loaf shape with buttered hands and place onto buttered baking dish, or pack into a buttered loaf pan. Bake about 40 minutes in a preheated oven (375°F). Serve with mushroom sauce. Serves four to six.

Shaker Boiled Fish

3-pound piece whitefish
OR fresh mackerel
1 quart water
2 tablespoons cider
OR white wine
½ teaspoon coarsely ground black
pepper
1 rib celery, chopped
1 large onion, sliced
2 carrots, sliced thinly
3 eggs

Remove head and tail from fish. Clean, skin, bone and wash if necessary. In a kettle, place water, wine, spice and vegetables. Bring to the boiling point, reduce heat and simmer 15 minutes. Add fish and simmer gently (170°F) for about 12 to 15 minutes if fish is in one piece, 8 to 10 minutes if not. Place fish on a hot platter and reheat 2 cups of the fish broth. Whisk the eggs to blend, and gradually pour the hot fish broth into them, in a thin stream, whisking constantly. Serve immediately. Since the sauce has a tendency to curdle, a modernized version of the Rich Fish Sauce (see Index) may be used.

Shaker woven baskets. A wide variety of baskets were made and sold by the Shakers. The small basket in the foreground came from Canterbury, N.H. The largest basket is called a field basket; a smaller general-use basket is resting inside it.

Flake tuna. Melt butter in saucepan over low heat and add flour to form a roux. Stir in milk gradually and cook until thickened. Remove from heat and gradually stir in tuna, eggs, pepper, lemon juice, onion, parsley, pimiento and olives. Pour mixture into a buttered 2-quart baking dish. Melt butter and stir in bread crumbs. Sprinkle on top of casserole and bake in a preheated 375°F oven for about 25 minutes, until top is nicely browned. Serves four.

Scrape fish well to remove scales. Clean, dress, remove head and tail and wash thoroughly. Use head and tail to make broth, if desired. Simmer the bass in salted water until it is tender, about 20 minutes. Remove from water and flake fish, taking care to remove all skin and bones. Add parsley, onion and celery to cream, and heat to simmer. Strain, reserving liquid. Melt butter in a saucepan over low heat. Stir in flour to form a roux. Add scalded cream slowly, stirring constantly until smooth. Butter a deep baking dish and place in a layer of fish and a layer of sauce. Repeat until dish is ⅔ filled. Cover top with a layer of bread crumbs and sprinkle with grated cheese. Bake in a preheated oven, 350°F for 30 minutes, until mixture is bubbling, and surface is nicely browned. Serves six.

VARIATION: A nice variation of the above recipe, and one of our lenten favorites, is to alternate layers of fish and cooked brown rice with the sauce. In that case, make an extra cup of sauce, so the finished dish is not dry.

Mary Whitcher's Shaker House-Keeper

SHAKER ADVICE ON COOKING FISH: "The heads, back-bones and tails of fish should be cooked with a dash of marjoram and thyme and salt for half an hour and the liquid used in making sauces for fish or chowders. Green onions and parsley stewed in butter and combined with two cups of fish broth and poured over two slightly beaten eggs make a delectable sauce for boiled and baked fish."

Scalloped Tuna

2 cups cooked or canned tuna, drained
2 tablespoons butter
4 tablespoons flour
1 cup milk, warmed
2 eggs, beaten
¼ teaspoon pepper
1 tablespoon lemon juice
2 tablespoons green onions, chopped
1 tablespoon parsley
1 tablespoon pimiento, chopped
2 tablespoons black olives, chopped
2 tablespoons butter
½ cup bread crumbs

Turbot in Cream

2- to 2½-pound whole bass
Salted water to cover
2 cups light cream
4 sprigs parsley
2 medium onions
3 ribs celery
2 tablespoons flour
4 tablespoons butter
½ cup dried bread crumbs
¼ cup grated cheddar cheese

SAUCES

*The Infirmary, Center Family,
North Union, Ohio*

SAUCES

No cook is really good without a lively imagination and the will to use it.
— Sister Lisset.

In 1888, a Cincinnati woman wrote of a visit she and her family had paid to the Shakers at Mt. Lebanon, New York. Though their visit had been unexpected, the Shakers received them kindly. What made the greatest impression on the lady from southern Ohio, however, was the food laid before them.

"I will simply say that I never understood before to what perfection the art of cooking can be brought," she wrote. "Now, I want you to get my exact meaning. There was nothing 'rich' about the meal in the English or French sense; it was 'plain' cooking made delicious to the palate, tempting to the eye, and, as we found, in the highest degree digestible and nutritious."

Delicious to the palate and tempting to the eye: this was Shaker cooking at its best. Though "plain," it was never drab. Helping make it so were a variety of sauces used with both main and dessert dishes.

Brandied Hard Sauce

½ cup butter
1 teaspoon dark rum
1 tablespoon brandy
2 to 3 cups powdered sugar

Cream the butter until creamy and fluffy. Add the brandy and rum, and cream again. Add powdered sugar a little at a time, creaming well after each addition until a stiff consistency is achieved. Some people like the sauce at a spreading consistency, while others prefer it stiff and almost crumbly. Use just enough sugar to achieve the desired result. Pack into a bowl or jar. Cover tightly, and let ripen for a few hours or overnght in the refrigerator to blend flavors. Makes a generous cupful.

A version of this recipe was probably used by the early Shakers before the ban on the use of alcohol announced in 1828.

Sister Jennie's Shaker Desserts

Cider Sauce

1 tablespoon butter
2½ teaspoons flour
3 cups cider concentrate
2 to 3 tablespoons sugar or honey

Evaporate cider by simmering until reduced to half of its original volume. Melt butter over low heat and blend in flour. Add hot cider gradually, stirring until it is smooth and begins to thicken. Stir in sugar or honey and simmer 5 minutes. Serve hot. Makes 1½ cups.

Shaker Cider Concentrate

1 gallon fresh apple cider

In a large, non-metallic pot, simmer the cider until it is reduced to about 5½ to 6 cups. Pour into a sterilized jar, cover and refrigerate until needed.

Frozen concentrated apple juice may be substituted for the cider concentrate in any recipe.

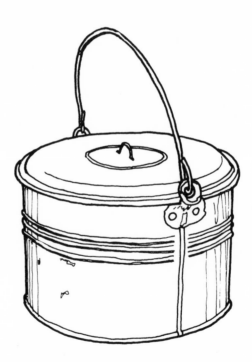

Tin bucket used for picking berries. Thought to be from Canterbury, N.H.

AN ANCIENT ART: Cider-making is an ancient and simple process. The juice was pressed from the crushed fruit, after which it was passed through a straw sieve and run off into barrels. The barrels were then placed in a cool cellar where, after the bung was removed, time and nature did the work. After the Shakers advocated total abstinence, they pasteurized the sweet cider rather than use chemicals to prevent fermentation.

Melt butter in a saucepan over low heat. Stir in the flour thoroughly, so flour does not lump. Slowly add stock, a little at a time, stirring constantly until thickened and smooth to form a velouté. Stir in wine or cider and return to a simmer. In the top of a double boiler, over hot water, beat egg yolks and cream together until just heated. Pour the velouté into the yolk-cream mixture in a thin stream, beating constantly with a whisk, rotary or electric beater until all veloute is incorporated and sauce is thickened and shiny. Serve immediately.

Boil water and sugar together until it reaches the soft-ball stage (236°F). Beat egg yolks and salt together. Beat in the vanilla. Pour the hot sugar syrup into the egg yolk mixture in a thin stream, beating constantly and vigorously until cooled. Carefully fold in whipped cream. Very good on any pudding.

The Shakers were avid users of fresh herbs, and when they were in season, a variety of delicious herb-flavored butters were made and used in place of plain butter in cooking and as a spread.

Place butter in a large bowl. With an electric mixer or hand whisk, cream the butter until light and fluffy. Gradually beat in the herbs. Pack into a crock or other container and chill. Use instead of plain unflavored butter. Make a variety of flavors, to use with fish, meat, vegetables, in sauces and as a taste-tempting spread for fresh, hot, homemade bread.

Fresh marjoram, summer savory, thyme, dill, chives, rosemary, and basil are especially delicious in this mixture. Dried herbs may be substituted for the fresh, but the results are not as dramatic. Substitute 1½ tablespoons dried herbs for the fresh and soak them in 4 tablespoons of warm water to reconstitute them.

Sister Content, North Union

Rich Fish Sauce

3 tablespoons melted butter
3 tablespoons flour
2 cups fish stock
¼ cup dry white wine or cider
3 egg yolks (reserve whites for Noodles. See Index.)
⅓ cup heavy cream

Shaker Foamy Sauce

½ cup water
1 cup sugar
2 egg yolks
½ teaspoon salt
2 teaspoons vanilla
1 cup whipped cream

Sister Content's Herb Butter

1 cup sweet butter
¼ cup finely chopped FRESH herbs

Horseradish Sauce

1 cup White Sauce
3 tablespoons freshly grated
  horseradish root
1 teaspoon sugar
2 tablespoons cider vinegar
⅛ teaspoon ground thyme
½ teaspoon dry mustard

The recipe for White Sauce appears later in this chapter. Heat White Sauce to simmering. Add remaining ingredients, and heat. Do not boil. Serve hot, with fish, simmered meat or vegetables.

Lemon Sauce

½ cup sugar
½ cup sweet butter
1 egg
1 teaspoon grated lemon rind
½ cup boiling water
Juice of one lemon
1/16 teaspoon nutmeg

Cream sugar and butter together. Beat in egg and lemon rind. Transfer to top part of a double boiler. Gradually add boiling water, stirring constantly. Heat over hot water in a double boiler for about 5 minutes, stirring occasionally. Stir in lemon juice and nutmeg. Serve hot.

Sister Jennie's Lemon Pie Filling

1½ cups sugar
¼ teaspoon salt
¾ cup flour
2 cups boiling water
4 egg yolks, room temperature
Juice and grated rind of 2 lemons
1 tablespoon sweet butter
¼ cup sugar

In the top of an enameled, glass or stainless steel double boiler, over hot water or in a non-metallic saucepan over low heat, stir sugar, salt and flour. Add boiling water slowly, stirring constantly and rapidly. Cook until thickened, stirring as needed to prevent lumping. Mixture should thicken fairly quickly. When thickened, pour slowly, in a thin stream, over the egg yolks and stir vigorously. Add lemon juice, rind, remaining sugar and butter, and return custard to boiler top. Place boiler top over hot water and continue cooking until yolks have thickened, about 5 to 8 minutes. Serve immediately.

There is more than one recipe for Shaker lemon pie. This one, which makes an excellent sauce, comes from a handwritten book of dessert recipes kept for many years by Sister Jennie M. Wells, a member of the Watervliet, N.Y., Mt.Lebanon, and Hancock societies.

Sister Jennie's Shaker Desserts

Maple Hard Sauce

⅓ cup butter
½ teaspoon maple flavoring
1 cup sugar, powdered

Cream butter until light and fluffy. Gradually cream in maple flavoring, then sugar, a little at a time. Form into balls, or squeeze through a pastry tube into fancy shapes; dust with nutmeg. Chill before serving. These may be made in quantities, and frozen indefinitely. When placed on warm dumplings or puddings, the sauce melts down slowly and mingles its delicate flavor with that of the dessert. Makes about ⅔ cup.

Mushroom Sauce

2 tablespoons butter
1 cup sliced, fresh mushrooms
1 tablespoon onion, minced
Salt and pepper to taste
¹⁄₁₆ teaspoon summer savory
1 tablespoon flour
1 cup vegetable, beef or fish stock

Place butter in skillet and heat over moderately high heat until butter is sizzling, but not browned. Sauté mushrooms and onion in the butter, to a very light brown, no longer than 5 minutes. Stir in flour to form a roux. Slowly add remaining ingredients, and cook until thickened. Serve hot. Makes 1½ cups.

Golden Mushroom Sauce

2 cups fresh mushrooms, sliced
3 tablespoons butter
2 tablespoons minced onion
2 tablespoons flour
2 cups half-and-half
Salt and pepper to taste
1 teaspoon parsley, minced, or ¼ teaspoon dried leaves

Sauté mushrooms in butter until slightly wilted. Add onion and continue cooking until lightly browned. Blend in flour to form a roux. Cook until flour is lightly browned. Gradually stir in half-and-half, and blend until smooth. Stir in salt, pepper and parsley. Serve hot. Makes about 3 cups.

AID FROM LEMONS: In 1881 *The Manifesto* published monthly by the Shakers approvingly quoted these words to its readers: "Lemon juice is the best anti-scorbutic [remedy for scurvy] known....I advise everyone to rub their gums daily with lemon juice to keep them in health. The hands and nails are also kept clean, white, soft and supple by the daily use of lemon instead of soap. It also prevents chilblains....Neuralgia may be cured by rubbing the part affected with a cut lemon. It is valuable also to cure warts....Natural remedies are the best, and Nature is the best doctor, if we would only listen to it."

Mustard Sauce

2 tablespoons butter
2 tablespoons flour
1 cup hot chicken stock
1 tablespoon prepared mustard
1 teaspoon dry mustard
¼ teaspoon salt
⅛ teaspoon pepper
1 teaspoon prepared horseradish

Over low heat melt butter and add flour to form a roux. Slowly stir in hot stock to form a velouté. Add remaining seasonings and serve immediately.

Pudding Sauce

1 cup sugar
2 tablespoons cornstarch
1/16 teaspoon salt
2 cups boiling water
2 tablespoons butter
Juice of one lemon

Mix sugar, cornstarch and salt in a non-metallic saucepan and add boiling water. Mix well. Add butter and cook 5 minutes. Remove from heat and stir in lemon juice. Serve very hot. Any flavoring may be added to this basic recipe, such as: 2 tablespoons rosewater, or ½ cup grape jelly, or 2 tablespoons of any fruit cordial, or ½ cup of frozen cider concentrate, or cider which has been evaporated by boiling to half its original volume.

Excellent Pudding Sauce

2 cups brown or maple sugar
2 tablespoons cornstarch
½ teaspoon salt
2 cups boiling water
2 tablespoons butter
2 tablespoons vinegar
1 teaspoon vanilla
⅛ teaspoon nutmeg

Mix sugar, cornstarch and salt. Add boiling water and boil for 5 minutes, stirring frequently. Blend in butter, vinegar, vanilla and nutmeg. Serve very hot.

THE MUSTARD CURE: With the faith in nature as the best physician, the Shakers made good use of mustard for curative as well as dining purposes. Mixed with warm water, it made an emetic, while a hot mustard foot bath was believed to avert a cold. A mustard plaster applied to a sick chest was also believed to be an effective remedy.

Cream butter with sugar. Stir in flavoring. Do not chill, for this will cool the pudding.

Soft Sauce

1 cup butter
2 cups maple or brown sugar
2 tablespoons rosewater or almond
  extract

Have all ingredients at room temperature before using. Beat egg white very stiff; fold in mashed berries and beat until light and fluffy. Then gradually add sugar and beat until mixture stands in soft peaks. Then add soft butter and continue beating until fluffy, light and airy. May be used as a topping for shortcake or as a delightful sauce for an otherwise plain cake. Makes about 1½ cups.

Sister Lottie, Canterbury

Strawberry Sauce

1 egg white
1 cup strawberries, well mashed
1 cup powdered sugar
2 tablespoons soft butter

Cut tomatoes in quarters. Place in saucepan with cloves and onion and simmer for 15 minutes. Strain through a sieve. If canned tomatoes are used, omit straining. In a saucepan, melt butter and add flour to form a roux. Return strained tomatoes to the simmering point. Pour roux into simmering tomatoes and cook until slightly thickened, about 5 minutes more. Season to taste and garnish with parsley. Makes about 3 cups.

Tomato Sauce

8 medium-sized tomatoes or 4 cups
  canned stewed tomatoes
4 cloves
1 tablespoon onion, minced
2 tablespoons butter
1 tablespoon flour
Salt and pepper to taste
Few grains cayenne pepper
1 tablespoon parsley, minced

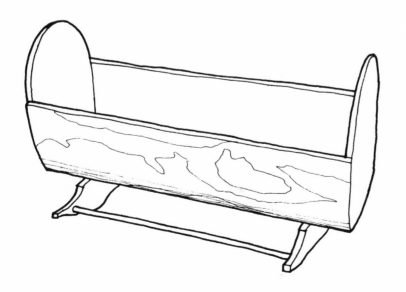

Cradle, 36″ long, with a railing which permitted a Shaker sister to rock it by a touch of the foot, while freeing her hands for other work.

Tasty Tomato Sauce

3 tablespoons butter
1 clove garlic, whole
1 large onion, minced
3½ cups tomato puree
8 sprigs parsley, or 2 tablespoons
  parsley flakes
1 sprig fresh thyme or ¼ teaspoon
  dried thyme
Tops of 4 ribs of celery, with leaves
Salt and pepper
1 teaspoon sugar

Heat butter and sauté garlic in it for 2 minutes. Remove garlic and add minced onion. Stir and cook until light browned. Add puree, parsley, thyme and celery. Season, and bring to the boiling point. Reduce heat to moderate, and simmer slowly for 20 to 25 minutes, stirring frequently to prevent scorching. Strain, and stir in sugar. Serve hot. Makes about 3¼ cups.

White Sauce

2 tablespoons butter
2 tablespoons flour
Salt and pepper to taste
1 cup warmed half-and-half
1 cup warm fish stock

Melt butter in a saucepan over low heat. Blend in flour, salt and pepper. Gradually blend in warmed half-and-half and stock. Cook about 5 minutes over low heat, stirring frequently. When serving this sauce on delicately flavored vegetables, substitute either water in which the vegetable has been cooked, or milk in place of the fish stock. Chopped hard-cooked eggs or shredded cheddar cheese may be added for variety.

RULES FOR EATING: "Never eat or drink contrary to your own conscientious principles even though others may deride you."

"Never drink unless you are thirsty, and then nature's wholesome and healthful beverage [water] will be agreeable and delightful."—*The Manifesto*, 1885.

MORE RULES FOR EATING: "Never eat what you do not need because it pleases your taste. It is better to bear the cross and be saved from dyspepsia." "Never eat between meals."—*The Manifesto*, 1878.

VEGETABLES

The Meeting House, Center Family,
North Union, Ohio

VEGETABLES

Our bodies are the food we eat. There are definite laws of nutrition which should be studied and followed rather than man eating to please his palate. – The Manifesto.

Today, when nutritionists talk about how a well-balanced daily diet should include foods from the recommended basic groups, we begin to appreciate how well-balanced a diet the Shakers followed. Depending almost entirely upon the produce of their own land, the Shaker sisters turned the raw material of their gardens, orchards, cellars and larders into dishes which would give strength and health to the Order and also be eaten with real relish and satisfaction by the members. Here in rural Ohio the Shaker records show that lemons and a few spices and an occasional keg of molasses were the only food products purchased from the outside markets of "The World."

In Shaker catalogs, the choices of seeds were legion for that day: endive, six kinds of squash, eight varieties of beans and as many peas, several sorts of both white and yellow sweet corn, and members of the melon family ranging from luscious watermelons to tiny citrons for preserving. The great cabbage family is described in the catalogs too: red and white varieties, sprouts, kohl, collards, greens of many sorts and mustard, in addition to a vast assortment of root vegetables.

Producing such a cornucopia of vegetables, along with a variety of herbs, kept the Shakers close to the core of nature. They toiled steadily through the growing season. In one of the Shaker farm journals, a Believer wrote, "Vegetables and fruits, when properly cultivated and prepared as they are freshly gathered, excel in flavour and nourishment. *Do not be content with one planting;* peas, beans, cucumbers, lettuce, spinach, corn and tomatoes and potatoes can be planted as late as the second week in August and yield before the frost sets in...."

As late as 1848 "land scurvy" was still a prevalent disease in America. Then the medical profession began to realize that the ailment was due to lack of fresh vegetables and fruits in the average diet. The Shakers helped bring about a greater use of these necessary foods in American cuisine.

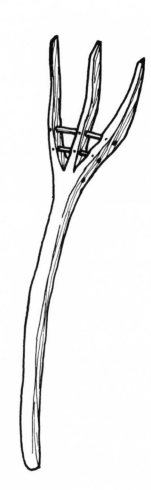

Wooden pitch fork.

Shaker Asparagus

1 pound asparagus stalks
1 cup boiling water
½ teaspoon salt
⅛ teaspoon sugar
1 sprig mint
2 tablespoons butter
¼ cup light cream
2 egg yolks
4 slices toasted bread, buttered
1/16 teaspoon nutmeg

With a vegetable peeler, peel the tough skin from each stalk of asparagus to about ⅓ from the top. Break off tops and break remainder of stalk into one-inch lengths. Place all but tops into boiling salted water and simmer 15 minutes, or steam in a steamer basket over simmering water 15 minutes. Drain, reserving ¼ cup liquid. Replace asparagus to saucepan and add seasonings, reserved cooking liquid, butter, cream, mint and asparagus tops. Simmer gently 10 minutes. Beat egg yolk and stir into cream mixture. Simmer 1 minute to heat. Turn out on buttered toast and sprinkle with nutmeg. Serves 4.

Amelia's Shaker Recipes

Shaker Baked Beans

4 cups dried navy or pea beans
2½ cups warm water
1 medium onion, whole, peeled
½ cup dark molasses
½ cup butter
1 teaspoon salt
2 teaspoons dry mustard
½ cup catsup or chili sauce

Place beans in a bowl and pour water over them. Cover and refrigerate overnight. Drain, and simmer in fresh water until tender (about 30-40 minutes after water starts to simmer). If time is short, add ½ teaspoon baking soda to beans and water and let stand at least 2 hours. Simmer in the same water until tender (about 35-45 minutes after water starts to simmer). Drain beans and reserve liquid. Place onion in bottom of a well-buttered, 2½-quart bean pot or deep casserole, and pour in beans. Add remaining ingredients to reserved liquid and pour over beans. Cover and cook in a preheated, very slow oven (250°F) for 3 hours. Add more liquid whenever surface appears dry. Remove cover for last half hour, raise oven temperature to 300°F, and brown surface well. Makes 10 to 12 side dish servings.

This excellent recipe for baked beans was used during the Shaker ban on pork. Several older Shaker "receipts" for this dish call for "medium thick slices of salt pork laid in the bottom of the bean pot which [will] gradually work their way to the top and flavor the entire contents of the pot." When salt pork was used, the butter was omitted.

Sister Josephine, Canterbury

WHEN TO CUT ASPARAGUS: Called "sparrow grass" long ago, asparagus was brought to America from Holland in 1786. The Shakers believed that it is time to cut asparagus when is only half an inch high, using a sharp knife and cutting several inches below the surface. It is then very tender and bleached.

Corn Oysters

2 egg yolks, slightly beaten
2 cups fresh corn, grated from the cob
½ teaspoon salt
¼ teaspoon black pepper
¼ cup all-purpose flour
3 egg whites, stiffly beaten

Mix all ingredients except egg whites together. Fold in beaten whites. Drop by serving spoonfuls (the size of an oyster) into a well-greased skillet. Brown on both sides and serve at once. Makes about 12. A very nice side dish with cold meat.

Fresh Corn Pudding

2 cups fresh corn, grated off the cob
3 eggs, lightly beaten
¼ cup sugar
¹⁄₁₆ teaspoon nutmeg
½ teaspoon salt
⅛ teaspoon black pepper
2 cups light cream
¼ cup buttered bread crumbs

Place grated corn in buttered 1½-quart baking dish. Mix together remaining ingredients. Blend well and pour over corn in baking dish. Sprinkle top with Buttered Bread Crumbs (explained below) and place in a pan of boiling water so water level is even with the level of the soufflé in the baking dish. Bake in a preheated slow (250°F) oven for about 1 hour, until set. Serves 6. May be served as a starchy side dish, or as a meatless main dish.

Amelia's Shaker Recipes

Buttered Bread Crumbs

1 cup dry bread crumbs
¼ cup sweet butter

In a saucepan or skillet, melt butter. Add bread crumbs and stir over low heat until butter is thoroughly absorbed. May be stored, refrigerated, in a covered jar until needed. Keeps 1 to 2 months.

THE MOST VALUED FOOD: Long ago, a North Union Shaker wrote in the society's annals: "Corn was our most valued single article of food. It not only fed our members in the early days, but also our cattle and hogs. In season we ate it from the cob thrice daily. What was left we cut from the cob and dried for winter use. In the early days we dried it on sheets in the sun but in later years we had a drying house where small wood-burning stoves furnished a gentle heat. We dried hundreds of pounds of corn in this fashion every year. Whatever was not consumed by our large household was sold in the neighboring markets by our peddler." At one time, in fact, drying sweet corn was the chief industry of the sisters at North Union.

Roasting Ears of Corn

12 ears sweet corn
Butter, salt, pepper

Carefully pull down husks from 12 ears of freshly picked corn. Remove the silk and replace the husk. Tie, if necessary, to hold together. Place in a preheated, slow (300°F) oven for 30 minutes. Serve as they are, or remove husks to serve. Be sure plenty of butter, salt and pepper is available.

This rule may be varied by removing all the husks before boiling, then placing a handful of sweet inner husks in the bottom of the kettle. This greatly enhances the flavor of the corn and is far simpler than removing the husks from the very hot ear.

Shaker Dolmas

2 quarts grape leaves (see note)
1 cup rice, uncooked
½ cup onions, chopped
2 tablespoons soft butter
½ teaspoon salt
¼ teaspoon pepper
½ teaspoon dried oregano
2 teaspoons parsley, minced
2 cups stock, boiling

Blanch grape leaves in boiling, lightly salted water for 2 minutes. Spread them out on a board to cool. Mix all ingredients together, except stock, and place 1 tablespoonful on each leaf. Roll each leaf, tucking in the edges to seal. Place extra leaves in the bottom of a dutch oven or other heavy covered saucepan. Arrange grape leaf rolls (dolmas) on them and cover with remainder of leaves. Place a heavy inverted plate on top of the dolmas and pour in the stock. Cook slowly, covered, until all liquid is absorbed, about 25 to 30 minutes. Serve very hot. Makes about 12 small or 6 large dolmas.

It is not known how this dish, which came from the Near East, entered Shaker cookery. However, the Shakers cultivated large vineyards near North Union and apparently learned to appreciate the tasty grape leaves.

NOTE: If grape leaves are not available, substitute chard, kale, or escarole leaves.

THE BANNING OF MEAT: During the ten-year interim of Shaker spiritualism (1837-1847), a ban was placed on meat eating by the head ministry at New Lebanon. Meat had become almost the chief item of diet in this new land; often three, four or even more kinds were served at a single dinner, while fruits, vegetables, cereals and milk products were sadly neglected in the average diet.

Although the great Shaker leader Elder Frederick Evans of New Lebanon, New York, looked forward to a day when all peoples would be vegetarians, the ban on meat eating was never strictly enforced throughout Shakerdom; it was left to the discretion of each member to decide for himself. In some communities separate tables were set for those who were vegetarians and those who ate meat.

Shaker Green Beans

2 pounds fresh green beans
6 slices bacon, chopped
1 cup boiling water
1 teaspoon sugar
½ teaspoon salt
1/16 teaspoon pepper
½ cup heavy cream

Break ends off beans and break beans into 2-inch lengths. Soak in cold water for 10 minutes. Sauce bacon in a heavy non-metallic skillet or skillet with a non-stick surface. When lightly browned, add beans and boiling water. When it returns to boil, lower heat and simmer 20 minutes. Drain. Add sugar, salt, pepper and cream and return to simmer for 5 minutes. Serve very hot.

Baked Greens

2 pounds fresh spinach, cress and
    mustard greens, mixed
6 slices bacon
½ medium onion, minced
1/16 teaspoon nutmeg
¼ teaspoon salt
⅛ teaspoon pepper
4 eggs
Salted water to cover

Wash and pick over greens carefully. Simmer, covered, until leaves are wilted, 10 to 12 minutes in only the water that clings to the leaves. Blendorize or process a few seconds. Pan broil bacon until crisp. Remove bacon, crumble into bits, and reserve. Sauté onion in bacon fat until tender. Add greens, bacon bits, salt and pepper. Reheat. Gently poach eggs in salted water. Turn greens mixture into serving plate and make 4 "wells" in the mixture. When eggs are ready, slip one poached egg into each "well." Dust each egg with nutmeg. Makes 4 servings..

North Union

A CROP FOR ALL REASONS: In the newly turned sod of the Midwest the European grains, such as wheat, barley and rye, were slow in getting started; corn alone yielded a fair harvest. Especially in the Ohio, Kentucky and Indiana Shaker communities, the pioneer Believers worked from dawn to dusk to eke out a scant existence. With the many strangers within their gates and constant visitations by their spiritual leaders from the East, the food problem was a constant one.

In his history of the Shakers of Ohio, MacLean wrote: "At first (early 1800s) it was Lent with them most of the time. Meat with them, as in all pioneer localities, was very scarce and most of the time they were without milk for their large families. Bread was also generally lacking; Indian bread and corn was their chief diet." Not only was corn the staple diet among the western Shakers in the early days and for many years which followed, they stuffed their ticks with its husks, they used it to make braided rugs for their thresholds, they fed it to their cattle and hogs, and they made corncob pipes for their old men and cornhusk toys for their children. The dried cobs also furnished them with fuel.

Shaker Hominy Cakes

2 cups canned or frozen hominy (not grits) or whole kernel corn
2 eggs, beaten slightly
1 teaspoon salt
1 teaspoon sugar
1 cup whole wheat flour
2 cups milk

Hominy Cakes are also known as Corn Fritters. Mix all ingredients together to form a batter. Drop by spoonfuls or small ladle onto a hot (385°F) buttered griddle or skillet. Brown on both sides to a rich golden color and serve with dinner in place of starchy vegetable. Makes an excellent change for breakfast when served with plenty of butter and syrup. Makes a total of 12 to 15 of these 2 1/2-inch fritters.

Mushrooms and Chestnuts

1 pound chestnuts
2 tablespoons butter
1 pound mushrooms, quartered
2 tablespoons flour
1½ cups light cream
½ teaspoon salt
⅛ teaspoon pepper
1 tablespoon parsley, minced

Cut an X-shaped slit in chestnut shells with the tip of a paring knife. Cover chestnuts with cold water and bring to boiling point. Reduce heat and simmer for 15 minutes. Drain, remove shells and skin, and cut into quarters. Heat butter in skillet over moderate heat and saute mushrooms until lightly browned. Blend in flour to form a roux. Slowly stir in cream, seasoning and nuts. Stir to heat thoroughly and thicken. Garnish with chopped parsley. Serve with hot corn bread or baked potatoes. For variety, add ½ cup shredded cheddar cheese to cream mixture. Serves 3 to 4.

Amelia's Shaker Recipes

How Hominy Was Made: In the early days, the Shakers made large quantities of hominy, a staple on the frontier. Making hominy was a lengthy procedure, for the corn had to be soaked in lye water overnight after it was shelled. The following morning it was boiled for three hours in the water in which it had been soaked. The corn was then washed and rubbed until the hulls came off, when it was again boiled and drained, and boiled and drained for yet a third time. A teaspoon of salt per quart of water was added to the last boiling. Hominy is made from white corn; "hulled corn" is made from yellow corn.

A Sauce for Vegetables: In their recipes, the Shakers suggested that delicately flavored vegetables, such as asparagus, chard or green peas, are best served with a white sauce made half with milk and half with the water in which the vegetable had been cooked. Thickened milk and cream are often too heavy and can destroy the flavor of the vegetable.

Shaker Noodles

1 cup bread flour
½ teaspoon salt
1 tablespoon soft butter
1 egg or 2 egg yolks
3 tablespoons water (see variations)

Sift flour into mixing bowl or onto a cutting board. Form a well in the center of the flour and place, in order, butter, egg, water and salt. Stir to combine ingredients, and if not already on a board, turn out onto a lightly floured board and knead until a smooth, stiff dough is formed (about 5 minutes). Divide the dough into three portions and roll each ⅛″ thick. Sprinkle surface with flour, turn over and sprinkle the other side. Place rolled dough on a clean, dry dish towel and let air dry while rolling the other two pieces. Allow each piece to dry for about 15 minutes.

Roll each dried piece of dough into a cylinder, jelly-roll fashion, and slice into wide, medium or fine widths, with a very sharp, non-serrated knife. Shake out each slice to separate and place on a towel to continue drying while you repeat the process with the remaining dough. Drop into rapidly boiling salted water and boil for about 5 to 7 minutes. Besides using for creamed dishes and as an accompaniment for stews and soups, these noodles may also be tossed with onions that have been sautéed in butter, and used instead of potatoes. Makes 4 servings.

NOTE: Bread flour is higher in gluten (wheat protein) than all-purpose flour, and so is better for making noodles. The texture of the noodles is firmer than with all-purpose flour. If bread flour is not available, omit water in the noodle recipe and add an egg white instead.

VARIATIONS: To add color, flavor and extra nutrition to the noodles, use the water in which vegetables have been cooked; or the cooked, pureed vegetables themselves instead of the water in the noodle recipe. Spinach, carrots and beets are especially good, while parsnips, turnips and mustard greens, may be used with highly seasoned dishes.

Mary Whitcher's Shaker House-Keeper

"THE COMPLETE FOOD": In 1834 Daniel Frazer, a man endowed with a vigorous intellect, joined the Shaker ranks. Dietetics and hygeine were his special interests; he was a practical chemist and consequently was of great service to Shakerism in the days when the vegetarian philosophy, of which both he and Elder Frederick Evans were ardent adherents, was being established on a practical basis.

Elder Daniel worked especially upon the value of milk and its products in diet, which today modern scientists declare to be an almost "complete food." Several of the Shakers were willing to prove Elder Daniel's theories about the great value of milk as a food, and for a year went on a "milk diet." Elder Daniel Offord, one of the most skilled mechanics and inventors among the Mt. Lebanon Shakers, lived on this diet with excellent results. All three of these reformers were strict vegetarians who maintained good health and lived to enjoy the rich fruits of old age.

Nut and Rice Patties

Fat for frying
1 cup chestnuts, cooked and chopped
½ cup dry bread crumbs
2 cups cooked brown rice
3 eggs
1 teaspoon parsley, chopped
½ teaspoon savory leaves
2 tablespoons light cream
½ cup flour

Heat fat in a skillet or fryer over moderate heat to a temperature of 360°F. Mix nuts, crumbs, rice, 2 eggs, parsley savory and cream. Shape into 8 patties. Dredge in flour, then into 1 beaten egg, then into flour again. Fry to a rich brown. Serves 4.

Union Village

Scalloped Onions

6 medium onions
¼ cup butter
⅓ cup bread crumbs
½ teaspoon salt
⅛ teaspoon pepper
2 tablespoons heavy cream
¼ cup grated hard cheddar cheese
1/16 teaspoon paprika

Skin and slice onions in thick slices. Melt butter in a non-metallic or stainless steel skillet, or skillet with a non-stick surface. Sauté onions until tender. Place in a buttered 1½-quart baking dish and stir in cream. Sprinkle with a mixture of crumbs, salt, pepper, cream, cheese and paprika. Bake in a 375°F oven until crumbs are browned. Serve very hot. Makes 4 servings.

North Union

NUTTING ON THE HEIGHTS: Chestnuts were most plentiful on the Heights near Cleveland where the North Union Shakers dwelt, as were black walnuts and hickory nuts. All three of these tasty nuts added their rich flavor to many a Shaker dish, especially during the meatless era of Shakerdom.

Not a single nut went to waste on the large Shaker estates. Chestnuts were very plentiful in the early days and were used by the Shakers in many ways—in stuffings, plain roasted and made in sundry combinations with eggs, rice and mushrooms. After the first frost in the autumn, the Shaker children were up before dawn to gather their precious harvest before the squirrels garnered them. After drying them in their attics, the hickory, butternuts and walnuts were cracked by the children. Quantities of them were consumed as a treat at Christmas time while other great quantities were fashioned into cakes, candies and cookies.

Stuffed Onions

6 large yellow onions
1 cup cooked veal or chicken
1 cup celery, minced
1 cup grated fresh corn
2 tablespoons pimento, chopped
½ teaspoon paprika
2 tablespoons heavy cream
1 teaspoon salt
⅛ teaspoon pepper
1 cup stock or broth
1 tablespoon butter

Skin onions and boil whole for 10 minutes in an enameled, glass or stainless steel saucepan. Core the centers with a spoon or melon-baller, and chop finely. Make a stuffing of meat, vegetables, cream and seasonings. Stuff onions with this mixture. Place in a buttered 3-quart baking dish, moisten each onion with stock, and dot with butter. Bake in a preheated moderate (350°F) oven for 20 minutes. Serves 6.

Amelia's Shaker Recipes

Parsnip Stew

8 parsnips
6 small, whole potatoes
3 small onions, sliced
Water
8 slices bacon
Salt and papper to taste

Simmer whole parsnips, potatoes and onions for 20 minutes in water to cover. Drain, reserving liquid. When vegetables are cool enough to handle, slip off skins and cut into thick slices. Place half of bacon in the bottom of a 2½-quart baking dish. Add a layer of vegetables, one at a time, and season. Repeat layering with bacon and vegetables. Fill dish to two-thirds with "pot liquor" and bake for 30 minutes in an oven preheated to 300°F. Serves 6 to 8.

Sautéed Parsnips

8 medium parsnips
¼ cup butter, melted
2 tablespoons flour
½ teaspoon salt
1 teaspoon sugar
Butter for frying

Scrape parsnips and cut into halves, lengthwise. Steam for 25 to 30 minutes in a steamer basket over simmering water, to retain delicate flavor. Dip them into melted butter and then into flour. Fry in moderately hot butter until they are delicately brown. Sprinkle with combined salt and sugar. Makes 6 servings.

North Union

THE ONION CURE: *The Manifesto* published monthly by the Shakers carried many articles about onions. Some argued for the curative value of the onion, benefits which modern science unfortunately has failed to demonstrate. In one such essay, in an 1881 issue of the Shaker magazine, it was asserted that "lung and liver complaints are certainly benefitted, often cured, by a free consumption of onions, cooked or raw. Colds yield to them like magic. Don't be afraid of them. Taken at night, all offense will be wanting by morning, and the good effects will greatly compensate for the trifling annoyance."

Poor Man's Asparagus

2 pounds tender green onions
Water to cover
2 tablespoons flour
2 tablespoons butter
½ cup light cream
1 teaspoon salt
⅛ teaspoon pepper
1 teaspoon prepared mustard
2 egg yolks

Remove tops of green onions so as to leave them about 8 inches in length. Simmer in water for 10 minutes. Drain, reserving 1 cup of "pot liquor." Melt butter and add flour. Blend into a roux and stir in the reserved liquid. Add cream, salt, pepper and mustard, and continue cooking over low heat, stirring until smooth and thickened. Arrange onions on a heated platter. Beat some of the cream sauce into the egg yolks to prevent curdling. Then beat that mixture into remaining hot cream sauce and pour over vegetables. This is a very tasty spring dish. Serves 4 to 6.

The Manifesto

Sister Jennie's Creamed Potatoes

10 large cold boiled potatoes
¼ pound butter
3 cups light cream
1 teaspoon salt
¼ teaspoon pepper
Crumbled bacon bits

Skin and thinly slice the potatoes. Place butter over low heat in a heavy non-metallic or stainless steel skillet, or skillet with a non-stick bonded surface. When butter is melted, add cream and heat gently. Drop in the sliced potatoes and season. Simmer very slowly until all cream is absorbed, about one hour. Stir gently only once during cooking. Serve piping hot topped with a modern touch: crumbled bacon bits.

Sister Jennie Wells, Hancock

Stuffed Baked Potatoes I

Baking potatoes
Salt, pepper
Light cream, scalded
Paprika
Parlsey, minced
Butter

Bake the needed number of potatoes of equal size. When done, cut in halves lengthwise. Scrape out the interior; mash and season with salt, pepper, and scalded light cream. Beat until very fluffy and light. Return to potato shell and dot generously with butter. Dust surface with paprika and minced parsley. Place under broiler until well heated and surface has browned.

Amelia's Shaker Recipes

Bake potatoes in a hot (450°F) oven for about 40 minutes. Prick skin so they do not burst in the oven. Remove from oven and cut in half lengthwise. Scoop out the interior and pass through a ricer, food mill or "china cap" strainer. Add butter, salt, pepper and cream and whip until fluffy. Beat egg white to very stiff peaks and fold into the potato mixture. Pile into shell and dust with paprika and a sprinkling of cheese. Return to oven until golden brown and cheese has melted. Serves 6.

Amelia's Shaker Recipes

Stuffed Baked Potatoes II

3 large baking potatoes
1 tablespoon butter
½ teaspoon salt
⅛ teaspoon pepper
½ cup heavy cream
1 egg white
1/16 teaspoon paprika
½ cup shredded cheddar cheese

Steam or bake the squash in the hot water. Remove from shell when tender. Mash well and season with salt, pepper, syrup and nutmeg. Beat well and reheat before serving, or place into a buttered baking dish and place in a 350°F oven until heated through, about 20 minutes. Makes 6 servings.

Shaker Squash

4 pounds winter squash, (acorn, Hubbard, butternut, etc.)
1 cup hot water
½ teaspoon salt
½ teaspoon pepper
3 tablespoons butter
½ cup pure maple syrup
¼ teaspoon nutmeg

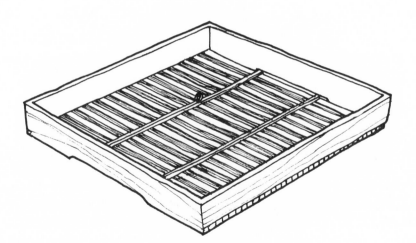

Winnow or bean sifter. The slat intervals can be adjusted to grade the size of the bean. Believed to have been made about 1858.

ADVICE ON SQUASH: Summer squash may be steamed or boiled, but do not pare or remove seeds. When tender, cut into pieces or pass through a coarse sieve and season well with salt, pepper, plenty of butter and a little cream. Place in a buttered baking dish in a moderate (375°F) oven to let surface brown. Most squash may be souffléed, baked, mashed, stuffed, pan-broiled, concocted into puddings and delectable puffs and pies.

Spinach with Rosemary

2 pounds fresh spinach
¼ teaspoon fresh rosemary, minced
1 teaspoon parsley, chopped
1 tablespoon green onion, chopped
2 tablespoons butter
Salt and pepper to taste
Sprinkling of nutmeg

Wash the spinach 3 or 4 times to rid it of all grit and sand. Pick off tough stems and bruised leaves. Chop or process until rather fine, and place in a heavy covered kettle. Add herbs and butter, and cover. Let simmer in its own juices until tender (about 15 minutes), stirring occasionally. Remove cover and add salt, pepper and nutmeg. Serve very hot. Serves 4

Amelia's Shaker Recipes

Sister Luella's Tomato Fritters

2 cups heavy tomato puree
1½ cups fine cracker crumbs
2 tablespoons minced onion
1½ teaspoons sugar
1 tablespoon flour
½ teaspoon salt
⅛ teaspoon pepper
3 eggs, beaten
3 tablespoons butter

Mix all ingredients together except butter. Heat butter in a skillet over moderate heat and drop in mixture by spoonfuls. Fry to a delicate brown. Serves 4 to 6.

TOMATOES AS AN AID TO "EFFICIENCY": An issue of *The Manifesto* in 1882 had this to say of tomatoes: "They are not, like milk, a perfect diet of themselves, and besides, like most other articles of food, they contain some obnoxious qualities. But they need not be thrown out on that account. Nature has provided us with such sufficient excretary organs that the obnoxious matter in our food, if in moderate amount, is readily cast out, and the body is protected against any material injury....A positive good may actually be derived from the use of food containing some such foreign matter, by way of giving increased activity and strength to the excretory organs from their exercise in casting such foreign from our bodies...."

SALADS &
SALAD DRESSINGS

The Mill Family Wagon Shed,
North Union, Ohio

SALADS &
SALAD DRESSINGS

There are many delicious treats awaiting you in the fields if you learn to recognize and use them. – From a North Union journal.

In their farm and household journals the Shakers often expressed delight with the simple gifts of fields and garden—the first tender sprouts of the dandelions, later the dock and mallow, the cress thriving along the brook. They gathered these greens and transformed them into palatable salads. They also used the tender tops of beets, turnips and radishes and converted them into tasty greens.

The Shaker annals do not list salads as a special course, but we find all sorts of suggestions on how to use cress, the several lettuces they raised, celery (which was used from root to leaf top), and onions ranging from shallots to leeks. The Believers raised large amounts of dandelions in their well-cultivated gardens, for not only were the young tender leaves used in salads and greens but the root also was highly valued for its medicinal properties.

Here are some ideas for successful salads:
• Rub a wooden salad bowl with a clove of garlic. Toss into it, well washed and dried, very young leaves of spinach, the inside tender stalks of celery, the flowers plucked from a head of cauliflower and baby carrots only two inches long. Add olive oil and red wine vinegar; sprinkle with salt and pepper.
• Skin six medium-sized tomatoes and chill. Slice them on a bed of crisp lettuce leaves and serve with favorite dressing. Some say this is the best of all salads.
• Slice red and white radishes on the slaw cutter and serve on lettuce leaves with a Boiled Dressing (described later in this chapter).
• Cucumbers want herbs, and they are excellent appetizers, *The Manifesto* tells us: "Do not wilt them before dressing, for it makes them look unappetizing. Try serving them freshly cut from the garden, peeled and cut and dressed with minced dill and salt and pepper."

Tin dipper with a sieve bottom, probably used as a skimmer to lift food from hot water.

Sister Lettie's Beet Salad

6 fresh beets
Boiling water to cover
4 small onions
2 tablespoons sugar
1 teaspoon salt
1 teaspoon dry mustard
½ cup cider vinegar
2 whole cloves
2 whole allspice berries
1 medium onion, sliced
2 green peppers, sliced
6 leaves Romaine
4 hard-cooked eggs

Cook beets in boiling water until tender. Chill thoroughly and slice. Slice onions thinly and place with beets, in a non-metallic or stainless steel bowl. Prepare a dressing by combining sugar, salt, mustard and vinegar. Heat to boiling point and pour over beets. Chill thoroughly. Add shelled, whole hard-cooked eggs and let stand overnight, or longer in the refrigerator. Remove eggs, and slice. Drain beet salad, reserve dressing, and arrange in center of dish on Romaine leaves and surround with rings of sliced onions and green peppers. Garnish with slices of egg and pour on reserved dressing. Serves six.

Cabbage Salad

½ cup heavy cream
2 tablespoons powdered sugar
1 teaspoon salt
¼ teaspoon pepper
2 tablespoons cider vinegar
1 quart thinly sliced or chopped cabbage
3 medium onions, peeled or thinly sliced
8 lettuce cups

Beat cream until frothy and it begins to thicken. Gradually add sugar, beating constantly until thickened. Add salt and pepper to vinegar and fold into cream. Toss cabbage with onions and fold in dressing. Pile into lettuce cups. Makes 8 servings.

Shaker Carrot Salad

2 cups carrots, cooked and diced
2 cups chestnuts, parboiled and diced
½ cup green peppers, chopped
6 lettuce leaves

Toss all ingredients, except lettuce, with Shaker Boiled Salad Dressing II (described later in this chapter). Pile onto crisp lettuce leaves and serve. Serves six.

Sister Melissa, Watervliet, Ohio

SALAD WISDOM: "To make a good salad four persons are wanted: a spendthrift to furnish the oil, a miser to measure the vinegar, a councillor to dole out the salt and spice, and a madman to toss it!"—*The Manifesto*.

Corn Salad

12 ears fresh corn
OR 6 cups frozen corn
Boiling water to cover
½ small head cabbage
4 sweet red peppers
1 bunch celery
¾ cup water
1½ tablespoons salt
1 cup cider vinegar
1 cup water
1 cup water
1½ tablespoons dry mustard
½ cup sugar

Cook corn on the cob for 7 minutes in boiling water. Remove from cob. Finely chop celery, cabbage and peppers. Add the ¼ cup water and steam for 10 minutes and drain. If frozen whole-kernel corn is used, add to celery, cabbage and peppers before steaming. Mix all vegetables with salt, vinegar, remaining water, mustard and sugar. Bring to a boil and cook 20 minutes. Place into hot sterilized jars immediately, and seal to preserve for later use, or chill before serving on a bed of lettuce. Makes about 4 pints, or enough for 16 salad-size or side-dish servings.

Union Village

Cucumber Salad

2 cucumbers
½ onion, thinly sliced
½ cup sour cream
¼ cup cider vinegar
½ teaspoon salt
¼ teaspoon pepper
2 tablespoons sugar
¼ teaspoon mustard

Select tender young cucumbers. Cut strips, lengthwise, from the skin. Slice thinly and toss with onions. Sprinkle with salt and let stand just three minutes. Drain thoroughly, pressing lightly to remove excess liquid. Prepare a dressing of sour cream, vinegar and seasonings and pour over vegetables. Toss to combine well. Serve at once for full flavor. Serves 6.

Amelia's Shaker Recipes

A VALUABLE VEGETABLE: *The Manifesto* asserts, "It does not seem generally known that the cucumber is one of the most valuable vegetables we raise. It can be dressed in more palatable and suitable ways than most any other vegetable except tomatoes. It is far better than squash and more delicate than eggplant when stewed, fried or stuffed and is most delicious when made into fritters in a dainty batter. Even when they have become too old to be served as salad and too tough for pickling, it is then the cucumber is at its best for cooking."

SALAD HINTS FROM THE MANIFESTO: "Rings made from the whites of hard-cooked eggs are a nice garnish for salad."
    "Pick over and carefully wash your cress to remove all slugs and sand. Arrange in a deep dish and serve with spiced vinegar."

Fresh Fruit Salad

3 cups ripe pears, diced
3 cups ripe peaches, diced
1 cup tart, red apples, diced
1 cup seedless grapes
1 cup mayonnaise
1 cup heavy or sour cream
8 lettuce leaves

Pare the pears and peaches, but not apples, and cut into half-inch dices. ("Do not mince food for salads, for it looks very unappetizing after dressing is added.") Add grapes. Blend mayonnaise with cream and add to fruit. Serve cold on a bed of lettuce. Makes 8 servings.

Amelia's Shaker Recipes

Molded Fruit Salad

2 cups calf's foot jelly
2 cups canned pears, drained and diced
2 cups canned peaches, drained and diced
½ cups seedless grapes
1 tablespoon orange marmalade

Heat jelly just to liquify. If homemade jelly is not available, substitute 1 three-ounce package of lemon-flavored gelatin dessert mix. Heat the liquid from the canned fruit plus water to make 1½ cups. When hot, prepare dessert in the usual way, adding marmalade. Chill until thick and syrupy. Fold in fruit and pour into a five-cup mold. Refrigerate until firm. Unmold and serve with your favorite dressing.

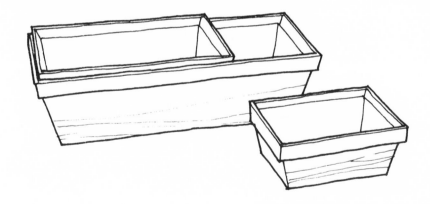

Wooden berry baskets.

Green Bean Salad

2 cups cooked, cut green beans
2 cups lettuce, shredded
2 whole green onions, chopped
2 sprigs summer savory, minced
6 nasturtium leaves
12 nasturtium pods
Salt and pepper to taste
Any favorite salad dressing

Mix the cold, cooked green beans with the shredded lettuce. Sprinkle the green onion over salad. Add the herbs and seasoning. Just before serving, toss with your favorite salad dressing. Serves four.

Amelia's Shaker Recipes

Cool potatoes just enough to handle; remove skins and slice thinly. Pan broil bacon until crisp. Crumble bacon and return to bacon drippings. Add onion, and sauté until translucent but not brown. Add salt, pepper, sugar and vinegar. Heat to simmering and turn this hot dressing immediately over warm potatoes. Toss lightly and place salad on a bed of lettuce. Sprinkle generously with parsley. Garnish with hard-cooked eggs. This dish is very satisfying when served with cold meat and cheese. Will serve six, amply.

Amelia's Shaker Recipes

Break fish into one-inch pieces. Add vegetables and seasonings. Moisten with Shaker Boiled Dressing I, and serve on lettuce. Garnish with sliced eggs. Makes 4 luncheon-size servings.

This is a basic boiled dressing.

Mix the dry ingredients and stir into well-beaten egg yolks. Add the liquids and stir well. Place in the top of a double boiler over low heat and cook until thickened. Add butter and let cool before using. This dressing is especially good on potato, cabbage or other vegetable salads.

VARIATIONS FOR USE ON FRUIT SALADS: (1) Beat in 1 cup of heavy or sour cream to cooled basic dressing; (2) Substitute orange or pineapple juice for vinegar and water. Substitute honey for sugar.

Amelia's Shaker Recipes

Shaker Potato Salad

6 medium potatoes, cooked in their jackets
3 slices bacon
1 medium onion, minced
½ teaspoon salt
1/16 teaspoon pepper
1 tablespoon sugar
½ cup vinegar
1 tablespoon parsley, minced
3 hard-cooked eggs, quartered
2 bunches leaf lettuce

Salmon Salad

2 cups canned or freshly cooked salmon
½ cup celery, diced
½ cup cabbage, shredded
¼ cup green peppers, shredded
1/16 teaspoon onion powder
½ teaspoon salt
⅛ teaspoon paprika
8 lettuce leaves
3 hard-cooked eggs, sliced

Shaker Boiled Salad Dressing I

¼ teaspoon dry mustard
1 teaspoon salt
1 teaspoon sugar
⅛ teaspoon pepper
1/16 teaspoon cayenne
3 egg yolks
½ cup each cider vinegar and water
1 tablespoon butter

Shaker Boiled Salad Dressing II

2 tablespoons butter
1 teaspoon salt
⅛ teaspoon cayenne pepper
2 teaspoons granulated sugar
2 teaspoons dry mustard
2 eggs
1 cup cider vinegar

Melt butter in the top of a glass, enameled or stainless steel double boiler over low heat. Add salt, pepper, sugar and mustard. Add eggs and beat well with a rotary or electric beater until light. Add vinegar a little at a time, beating constantly until thickened. Remove from heat and cool.

Sister Melissa, Watervliet, Ohio

Herb Salad Dressing

1 tablespoon minced onion
½ teaspoon salt
½ teaspoon dry mustard
⅛ teaspoon pepper
1 tablespoon minced thyme
1 tablespoon minced savory
3 tablespoons tarragon vinegar
6 tablespoons olive oil

Add vegetables, herbs and seasonings to vinegar. Beat in the oil. Serve immediately; dressing will separate. If fresh herbs are unavailable, substitute 1 teaspoon of the dried.

SUCCULENT GRUB: "Beets, cabbage, chard, chicory, endive, turnip leaves, dock and mustard all are very succulent grub when properly combined and dressed. Sour sorrel is another tasty plant one should not overlook for flavor in salads…Borage—its first tender leaves when added to salads awaken in one a new sense of joy that spring is again here!"—Gleanings from Shaker accounts.

SHAKER SALAD HINTS: *The Manifesto* suggests, "Salads should always be served as soon as possible after preparing them. Salads should be tossed or blended very lightly with a couple of wooden forks; never pack or mash them."

"To fringe celery, cut in four-inch lengths; stick several sewing needles into a cork and comb celery with it. Throw in very cold water to curl. This makes a pretty dish."

BREADS

The Grist Mill on Doan Brook,
North Union, Ohio

BREADS

Bread is the one food one can eat thrice daily and not tire of.
— A North Union household hint.

No one can well abstain from a meat diet unless he has good bread," wrote Sister Martha J. Anderson from the Mount Lebanon Shaker society in 1893. "We have three kinds on the table at each meal; white bread, also unleavened and leavened, made of unbolted wheat, which is washed and ground fresh at home every week."

More conscious than most people of their time of the connection between food and health, the Shakers made no secret of their preferences in regard to the staff of life. As early as 1871 various articles on bread appeared in *The Manifesto,* the official monthly magazine of the Shakers. These articles were chiefly protests on the milling of wheat; the millers, it was claimed, were separating and discarding the "live germ of the grain" in their attempts to make flour light in weight and color. The Shakers went so far as to say that "what had for countless ages been the staff of life had now become but a weak crutch!"

One such article was written by guest contributor Henry Ward Beecher, a passionate preacher and leading crusader for such causes as woman suffrage and the abolition of slavery. Wrote Beecher: "For thousands of years man has eaten without a scientific motive (but) today we are beginning to see we need muscle-building, nerve-replenishing, and bone-building food....The host of the future will, instead of asking a guest to take beef pudding and rich desserts, say to a lean, cadaverous visitor, 'Let me fill up your tissues,' or, 'My dear sir, your bones are brittle; therefore allow me to pass you some of this compound'—or, to some exigent scholar, thin and nervous, our host will say, 'My dear fellow, let me help you to some brains; this dish runs strongly to poetry, or is it philosophy you favor?' "

In its day this article might have sounded a bit exaggerated, but today we know that what people eat is intimately connected with their health and well-being. The Shakers caught sight of this truth long before home economics classes were taught in our schools and colleges. They understood that man does not live to eat but eats to live, and so they turned to Mother Nature for her store of natural foods—fruits, grain, vegetables, greens and herbs—for their sustenance in a day when people lived chiefly upon meats

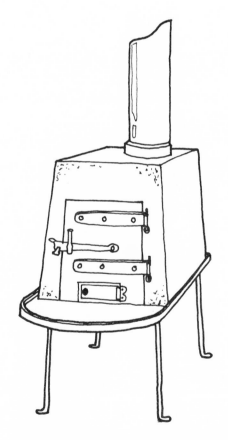

Box stove of the classic Shaker design was simple and efficient. One or more were found in every Shaker room.

and heavy sweets. Their "cattle upon a thousand hills" furnished them with the milk and milk products that today are considered the complete food. Moreover, they struggled to restore bread to its rightful heritage—the "staff of life"—by insisting that its live germ be retained in milling flour.

Much of the Shakers' wisdom on bread deserves respect today. But who could consistently obey Sister Laura's strict injunction of the time: "Wheaten loaf freshly taken from the oven should never be eaten while hot no matter how tempting it smells"?

YEAST BREADS

Sister Harriet's Coffee Cake

½ envelope or 1½ teaspoons dry
   activated yeast
1¼ cups 110°F water
4 cups all-purpose flour
¼ cup butter
3 eggs, slightly beaten
¼ teaspoon salt
½ cup sugar
2 tablespoons melted butter

Dissolve the yeast in warm water and add enough flour to knead into a soft ball with your hands. Drop this ball into a pan of warm water (110°F) to cover. Place a towel over the pan and let stand in a warm place for an hour. Heap the remaining flour on a board and form a well in the center with your hands. Into the well, place butter, eggs, salt and sugar. Knead this mass with your hands, gradually incorporating all of the flour, until a smoothly textured ball is formed.

Discard the water from the bowl in which the ball of yeast and flour have been rising, and knead this ball into the larger smoothly textured ball until it becomes smooth and elastic (about 30 times, or 4 minutes). Place into a buttered bowl and let rise in a warm place (about 100°F) until double in volume, or about 6 hours.

Punch the dough down, knead again about 20 times, and refrigerate for 12 hours. Remove from the refrigerator and press out dough into a shallow pan, 9″ by 10″ by 1½″ or 9″ by 12″ by 1″. Preheat oven to 400°F, and let the dough rise for about one hour at kitchen room temperature. Brush surface well with melted butter, and sprinkle generously with cinnamon topping or streussel topping. Bake 30 minutes at 400°F.

Sister Harriet Snyder was cook at the guesthouse at North Union. She was famous for her original dishes. This toothsome dish may sound like a lot of fuss and bother for a coffee cake, but we must remember that when Sister Harriet fashioned it, she probably multiplied this recipe by six. It is little wonder that some of the visiting elders recorded in their travel journals: "We sat down to a most satisfactory supper at North Union, every morsel of which we enjoyed."

Dissolve yeast in water to which the honey has been added. Scald milk with butter, sugar and salt and stir until well mixed. Cool until lukewarm, about 90°F. Stir in softened yeast mixture, and then enough flour to make a dough that will not stick to your hands. Knead the dough with the palms of your hands about 20 times. Place in a buttered bowl and brush the top with melted butter. Let rise to double its volume. Punch down, to remove excess gas and renew yeast activity. Knead lightly this time and shape into a loaf. Place in a greased and floured loaf pan, 9 inches by 4½ inches or equivalent, brush again with melted butter and let rise to double its volume.

Bake in a moderate (350°F) oven for about 50 minutes. Test loaf by tapping the top; if it sounds hollow, the loaf is done. Remove from pan immediately. Cover lightly with a towel to allow steam to escape. This is an excellent loaf of wholesome, crusty bread.

Sister Amelia, North Union

Dissolve yeast in the 4 tablespoons of water and stir in the 1 teaspoon sugar. Let stand for about 5 to 7 minutes. Beat eggs, adding sugar. Stir in salt and potatoes. Add dissolved yeast and enough flour to make a soft dough. Place in a buttered bowl and let rise for about 2 hours at 90°F.

Cream butter and remaining sugar together. Knead this into the dough by hand and let rise very slowly until double in volume (about 3 hours). Knead in, as before, warm water and place into a greased and floured 9″ by 4½″ loaf pan or a 9″ bundt pan. Let rise again until very light and high, and double in volume. Bake in a hot oven (450°F) for 15 minutes; lower heat to moderate (350°F) and bake until well browned (about 45 minutes).

North Union

Hints for Baking Bread: "Bread rises more quickly in the day time when the kitchen fires are kept going than at night when only embers smolder on the hearth; therefore four hours in the day time is equal to twelve hours of rising at night....In order to make really good bread, one must have well-milled flour. Use cast-iron bread pans if you want a good crusty loaf....The old brick oven with its even heat baked the best loaf."

Shaker Daily Loaf

1 envelope or 1 tablespoon dry activated yeast
4 tablespoons lukewarm water, 110°F
1 teaspoon honey
⅞ cup milk
1 tablespoon butter
2 teaspoons sugar
1 teaspoon salt
3 to 3½ cups sifted, unbleached flour
Melted butter to brush on top

Sister Jennie's Potato Bread

1 envelope or 1 tablespoon dry activated yeast
4 tablespoons water, 110°F
1 teaspoon sugar
2 eggs
¼ cup sugar
¼ teaspoon salt
1 cup boiled potatoes, mashed thoroughly
3 to 3½ cups bread flour, sifted
½ cup sweet butter
¼ cup sugar
⅞ cup warm water, 110°F

Shaker Sally Lunn

1 cup milk
3 tablespoons sugar
2 teaspoons salt
1 cup butter
1½ envelopes dry activated yeast
3 eggs, well-beaten
3 cups all-purpose flour
4 tablespoons melted butter
3 cups all-purpose flour (variable)

Scald the milk with the sugar, salt and butter. Cool to lukewarm (110°F) and sprinkle yeast into milk mixture. Stir in the well-beaten eggs. Beat in flour gradually, until batter is smooth. Let rise in a buttered bowl until double in volume. Knead in enough of the remaining flour to make a dough that is easily handled, and let rise again, until double in volume. Place in a greased and floured Sally Lunn pan, or a 10″ tube or Bundt pan. Brush surface well with melted butter and bake for 1 hour in a moderate (350°F) oven. Makes enough to serve 12 generous slices.

In the late 1700s in Bath, England, (the story goes) Sally Lunn sold buns and loaves fresh from the oven each morning and evening at a certain street corner. So delicious were they that the recipe still bears her name.

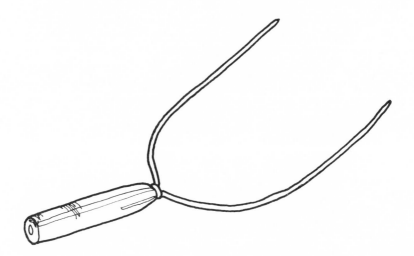

Bread lifter; metal with a wooden handle. Used to lift hot loaves.

NIGHT-RISING BREAD: In the days before factories produced most of the bread people consume, the Shakers and others set their dough in the evening and let it rise all night before the low embers of the open fire. This was the procedure at North Union, where at dawn the "Kitchen Sisters" could be seen lighting fires in the great brick ovens, getting ready for the day's bread-baking. After breakfast huge mounds of dough, which had slowly risen during the night and filled the ample dough trough, would be taken out and shaped into loaves. The kitchen records show that from twenty to thirty loaves were baked daily back in the days when a hundred Believers gathered thrice daily about the long tables at the Center Family Dwelling House.

Scald milk with butter and salt. Cool to 100°F. Dissolve yeast in 110°F water. Add yeast to cooled milk mixture and beat in first amount of flour to form a sponge. Cover and let stand overnight, at about 85°F. In the morning, add remaining ingredients, kneading in enough flour to make a dough that is not sticky, but is smooth, elastic and easy to handle. Cover and let rise in a warm place for several hours or until double in volume.

Shape into a loaf and place into a greased and floured 9" by 4 1/2" loaf tin or small bundt pan. Cover lightly, and let rise until double in volume. Bake in a preheated, moderate (350°F) oven for 50 minutes. Let cool slightly, about 10 minutes, and turn out onto a cake rack to cool. Dust surface with powdered sugar before serving.

Sister Lisset's Tea Loaf

1⅓ cups milk
¼ cup sweet butter
1 teaspoon salt
½ envelope or 1½ teaspoons activated
    dry yeast
2 tablespoons water, 110°F
2 to 2½ cups sifted unbleached flour
⅓ cup pure maple syrup
1 teaspoon cinnamon
½ cup raisins
½ cup currants
2½ to 3 cups sifted unbleached flour

Cinnamon-Sugar Topping

½ cup granulated sugar
2 teaspoons cinnamon
3 tablespoons flour

Blend all ingredients together. Keeps well in a tightly covered jar. Makes ½ cup.

Arthur Tolve's Streussel Topping

1 cup bread flour
1 tablespoon cinnamon
½ cup butter, unsalted
2 teaspoons almond extract
½ cup bread crumbs
½ cup granulated sugar
½ cup brown sugar, packed
1 teaspoon salt
⅔ cup bread flour
½ cup chopped walnuts or pecans

With your fingers, blend the first four ingredients. Add remaining ingredients and blend together by rubbing between the hands and fingers until the mixture resembles large to medium-size beans. Store in a tightly covered jar, in a cool place until required. Makes about 3 cups.

Shaker Wheaten Bread

1 cup milk
1 tablespoon salt
3 tablespoons honey or maple syrup
3 tablespoons butter
¾ cup water
1 envelope or 1 tablespoon dry
   activated yeast
¼ cup lukewarm water
1 tablespoon honey or maple syrup
4 cups whole wheat flour
2 cups unbleached white flour, sifted

Scald milk with salt, sweetener, butter and water. Let cool to about 100°F. Dissolve the yeast in the lukewarm water. Stir in sweetener and let stand for about 5 minutes until it becomes frothy. In a large bowl, add yeast mixture to cooled milk mixture. Stir in whole wheat flour, then enough white flour to make a dough that will not stick to your hands.

Turn out onto a lightly floured board and knead mixture until it becomes smooth and elastic, and does not stick to the board. Proceed as with Shaker Daily Loaf. Bake for 45 to 50 minutes in an oven preheated to 350°F. Yields 2 very substantial 8″ by 4″ loaves of extremely wholesome bread.

AN 1835 DINNER MENU: A North Union dinner menu from the travel journal of a visiting elder, dated July, 1835, reads as follows: "Cold mutton, fresh bread, hoe cakes, fried potatoes, turnip greens, peach preserves, Sally Lunn, tea and milk." The writer of the journal noted that the North Union Shakers were serving many meals to the host of Easterners who were migrating west in the 1830s.

THE VARIETY OF BREAD: Twenty kinds of breads are listed in the early Shaker recipe collections; among them, Wheaten Loaf, Injun (Indian) Bread, Dyspeptic Loaf, Whey, Rye, Brown, Boston, and Rutland Loaf. Many other kinds were named after the perfector of the loaf: Sister Lisset's Tea Loaf and Sister Jennie's Potato Bread, for example.

QUICK BREADS

Baking Powder Biscuits

2 cups all-purpose flour
½ teaspoon salt
1 tablespoon baking powder
¼ cup vegetable shortening
⅓ to ¾ cup milk
2 tablespoons melted butter

Sift flour, salt and baking powder together 3 times. Cut in shortening with pastry blender or two knives, scissors fashion, until mixture resembles coarse meal. Chill in the refrigerator for at least one hour.

Stir in milk with a fork to make a soft dough that leaves the sides of the bowl. Turn out onto a lightly floured board and knead gently about 10 times. Roll out to ¼" thickness and cut with a 1½" biscuit cutter. Place on a lightly greased and floured baking sheet without sides touching. Brush with melted butter and bake in a preheated 425°F oven for 12 to 15 minutes, or until tops are nicely browned. Makes about 12 biscuits.

Sister Lettie's Buttermilk Biscuits

2 cups all-purpose flour
½ teaspoon salt
1 tablespoon baking powder
½ teaspoon baking soda
3 tablespoons chilled butter
¾ cup buttermilk, chilled
3 tablespoons melted butter

Sift flour, salt, baking powder and soda together three times. Cut in the butter with a pastry blender or two knives, scissors fashion, until mixture resembles coarse meal. Chill the mixture in the refrigerator for about 1 hour or longer.

Add buttermilk and knead lightly, 10 to 15 times. Roll to ¼" thickness and cut with a 1½" round biscuit cutter, and place on lightly greased cookie sheet; or press the dough quickly into a shallow greased and floured pan 9" by 10" by 1½" and cut the dough into diamond- or square-shaped biscuits.

Brush with melted butter and bake 12 minutes at 450°F for round biscuits or at 400°F for 18 minutes for pan biscuits. Makes ten 2" or fifteen 1½" round biscuits. The pan biscuits will have tender, soft sides and must be separated. These biscuits are extremely light and delicious. There never seem to be enough!

EMERGENCY BISCUITS: The Shaker recipe for Baking Powder Biscuits can also be used for making drop biscuits. Just add 2 extra tablespoons of milk. Stir dough as little as possible and drop by spoonfuls on greased baking sheet. These are called quick or emergency biscuits, for they are very quickly made.

Cream Biscuits

2 cups bread flour
2 teaspoons baking powder
¼ teaspoon salt
1 cup heavy cream

Sift flour and baking powder together. Whip cream until stiff. Gently fold the flour into the cream until blended thoroughly. Turn out onto a lightly floured board and knead for one minute. Pat dough to ¼″ thickness and cut with 1½″ biscuit cutter. Arrange on a lightly greased and floured cookie sheet and bake in a preheated 450°F oven for 12 minutes. Makes 8 to 10 biscuits.

This dough also may be used for drop biscuits. In that case, do not knead, but drop by spoonfuls onto a greased and floured cookie sheet or into greased and floured muffin tins. Bake according to recipe directions.

These are also excellent for pot-pie toppings when cut in large circles, or as dumplings, when dropped into simmering stew!

Shaker Brown Bread

1 cup rye flour
1 cup yellow cornmeal
1 cup graham flour or whole wheat flour
1 teaspoon salt
1 cup lightly floured, chopped raisins
1¼ cups sour milk or buttermilk
¾ teaspoon baking soda
¾ cup molasses
2 tablespoons melted butter

Sift the first four ingredients together and mix well. In a bowl, combine the sour milk, soda, molasses and melted butter. Combine the two mixtures and stir thoroughly, adding the raisins. Pour into two buttered brown bread molds or 2 1-lb. coffee cans. Fill no more than two-thirds full. Tie buttered brown paper over the top of each coffee can.

Place containers on a rack in a large pot, taking care that simmering water does not touch the containers. Cover and steam for about 2 hours. Check water level at the end of one hour and replace if necessary. Remove from steamer pot, remove brown paper, and place containers in a pre-heated, 350°F oven for 30 minutes. Cool in the molds or coffee cans. To prevent the breads from drying out, do not remove from the mold until ready to serve.

Sister Laura, Canterbury, N.H.

BISCUIT HINTS FROM NORTH UNION: "Do not put the soda into the butter-milk or sour milk as most housewives have been accustomed to do in the past, for this immediately destroys the leavening power of the soda. Treat baking soda as a dry ingredient in baking."

"One cup of heavy sour cream can be substituted in a biscuit recipe for the butter and buttermilk. This recipe makes a splendid shortcake. At North Union we use the buttermilk biscuit recipe for pot pies. Buttermilk makes a far tastier and crustier biscuit than those made with sour milk."

1 cup yellow cornmeal
1 cup whole wheat flour
1 teaspoon salt
2 tablespoons sugar
½ teaspoon baking soda
2 teaspoons baking powder
1 cup sour cream
¼ cup milk
1 egg
1 tablespoon soft butter

Preheat oven to 400°F. Blend dry ingredients together and sift several times. Beat remaining ingredients together. Add to dry ingredients; stir until mixture is combined well. DO NOT BEAT. Turn out mixture into a shallow, buttered and floured 8″ square pan or 9″ cast-iron skillet and bake 20 minutes at 400°F. This makes a light, delicious corn bread. Serves 6.

Whitewater

Sister Lettie's Crullers

¼ cup sweet butter
1 cup sugar
3 eggs
1 teaspoon salt
1 teaspoon baking powder
¼ teaspoon nutmeg
¼ teaspoon allspice
3½ cups bread flour (approximately)
⅓ cup milk

Cream together butter and sugar. Cream in eggs, one at a time. Sift remaining dry ingredients together several times. Divide into four parts. Stir in each part alternately with three parts milk to creamed mixture, starting with flour and ending with flour. Form dough into a soft ball and let stand at room temperature 2 hours.

Roll out dough to ⅛″ thickness and cut into strips, 2 inches wide, with knife or wavy-edged pastry wheel. Cut across the strips on a diagonal, at 3-inch intervals to form diamond shapes. Make a 1″ long slash at the center, from long point to long point, to facilitate even frying. Fold one pointed end back through the hole in the center to form the classic "cruller twist."

Drop into oil that has been heated to 375°F and fry crullers to a golden brown. Sprinkle while hot with powdered sugar; or for variety, dredge in a mixture of ½ cup sugar and 2 teaspoons of cinnamon. These crullers are delicious, hot or cooled. Makes about 2½ dozen.

FOR MORE TENDER BISCUITS: "Chill butter before using in biscuits. This will give you a flakier and more tender hotbread. Do not give your dough when kneading more than eighteen strokes on a lightly floured board."

Dumplings

2 cups all-purpose flour
2 tablespoons baking powder
1 teaspoon salt
2 large eggs
¾ cup milk or half-and-half
  (variable)
2 cups meat or chicken stock

Sift flour with baking powder and salt. Break eggs into cup and fill with milk. Beat well and stir into dry ingredients. Heat stock in a large skillet or shallow braising pot, and bring to boil. Dip tablespoon into stock, fill with batter and drop into boiling stock. Do not cook too many at a time; they will stick together. Cover tightly and cook 2 minutes. Turn dumplings over and cook 2 minutes longer. Serve very hot with gravy, or cook mixture on the surface of beef or chicken stew. Makes 6 to 8 servings.

Sister Lettie's Gems (Popovers)

¾ cup bread flour, sifted
¼ cup unprocessed bran
2 tablespoons wheat germ
½ teaspoon salt
1 teaspoon baking powder
1 egg, beaten
¾ cup warmed milk, 120°F
2 tablespoons molasses

Sift the dry ingredients together and add beaten eggs blended with milk and molasses. Beat batter until light and foamy, and pour into very hot buttered "'gem" pans, that have been heated in a 425°F oven for about 15 minutes. Bake in a preheated oven, 425°F for 15 minutes, until brown and crusty.

Old Canterbury

A HOMEMADE BISCUIT MIX: We are sure that if refrigeration was as dependable and convenient as it is today, the Shakers' Baking Powder Biscuits could have been made into a mix; that is, all the dry ingredients sifted together and the butter or shortening cut in to the size of coarse meal. The mixture could then be stored indefinitely in a tightly covered jar or canister in the refrigerator or other cool, dry place and used by the cupfuls.

To use the mix, for every 2½ cups of mix stir in ¼ cup milk, and proceed with the recipe. The Baking Powder or Buttermilk Biscuit recipes may be tripled and kept refrigerated until required. Preserved in this way, the mix may be used for that "emergency," important event, or quick coffee cake. The biscuits are actually flakier if the dry mix is thoroughly chilled before adding the milk.

Sister Lisset's Graham Gems (Popovers)

1 cup Graham flour, or stone ground whole wheat flour
½ teaspoon salt
1 cup water

Combine all ingredients and beat 4 minutes if beating by hand, or 2 minutes on high speed with an electric mixer, until the bran in the flour has absorbed some of the water. Place greased and floured, cast-iron gem pans into a preheated 425°F oven for about 15 minutes, until grease is sizzling hot. (If gem pans are not available, small-cup muffin tins may be used, but heat only 7 to 8 minutes in a 425°F oven.)

Pour the mixture into the cast-iron pans and bake for about 15 minutes, or until the gems are brown and crusty. Because steam is the leavening agent, these gems will collapse readily if not served immediately. Makes about 1½ cups of batter, enough for 6 gems, ¼ cup in each.

SISTER LISSET'S QUAINT RULE: Sister Lisset left behind many recipes, among which is one for Graham Gems—which sounds like a tempting Sunday morning dish. Her quaint rule reads: "Stir whatever amount of graham flour your need calls for, into the right amount of cold water, making batter that is a trifle thicker than that used for griddle cakes. The secret of success in making tempting gems lies in the mixing: you must stir them rapidly and incorporate as much air into the batter as possible in the four minutes it takes to beat them up. Have your iron gem pans in the oven and have them good and hot and well buttered before pouring the batter. Bake them in a hot oven twenty minutes."

SYRUP AND GEMS: From the Shakers at Union Village, Ohio, came this household hint: "Serve gems on Sabbath morning with plenty of butter and maple syrup." The Shaker communities which made maple syrup usually opened a two-gallon jug of this luscious commodity each Sabbath for breakfast.

SISTER LISSET'S BISCUIT HINTS: "If you do not wish to light your oven on a hot day, bake your biscuits on a hot griddle. Grease lightly and place biscuits a good inch apart. Brown on one side for 5 minutes, turn, and brown on the other side. Very good biscuits!"

"An almost endless variety of biscuits can be made from any standard recipe by adding grated cheese, minced fruit, berries or spices. No cook is really good without a lively imagination and the will to use it!"—Sister Lisset.

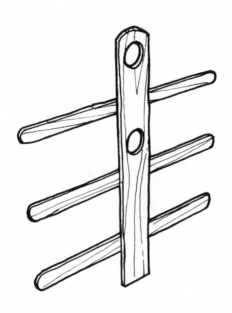

Multiple garment hanger.

Indian Griddle Cakes

1 cup cornmeal
2 cups buttermilk
1 cup all-purpose flour
½ teaspoon salt
1 teaspoon baking powder
2 egg yolks
2 egg whites
2 tablespoons melted butter

Stir cornmeal into buttermilk, and let stand about 20 minutes. Sift remaining dry ingredients together. Add yolks and butter to buttermilk mixture, and stir in dry ingredients to form a batter. Beat egg whites until stiff peaks are formed and fold carefully into batter. Bake on a hot (385°F) griddle. A soapstone griddle greased with a ham rind makes the tastiest griddle cakes. Fry to a rich brown. Cornmeal requires longer frying than wheaten cakes. Makes 8 generous cakes.

Watervliet, Ohio

Shaker Johnny Cake

2 cups cornmeal
½ teaspoon salt
1 teaspoon baking soda
1 cup sour milk or buttermilk
½ cup molasses
1 cup beef suet, finely chopped
OR ½ cup chilled butter or lard, cut
   into "bits"

Sift cornmeal, salt and soda together several times until well blended. If butter or lard is used, "cut" it into the dry mixture with a pastry blender, or with two knives, scissors fashion, until mixture resembles coarse meal. Stir in sour milk and molasses which have been mixed together. If beef suet is used, fold in last. Bake in a greased and floured, shallow 8" by 8" square pan or in a 9" round cast-iron skillet, 30 minutes in an oven preheated to 400°F. Serves 6 to 8.

Whitewater

Sister Hattie's Huckleberry Muffins

2 cups all-purpose flour
¼ teaspoon salt
4 teaspoons baking powder
3 tablespoons sugar
1 egg
1 cup milk
2 tablespoons butter, melted
1 cup huckleberries or blueberries
   tossed with 2 tablespoons flour

Sift the dry ingredients together and stir well to mix. Beat egg with milk and melted butter. Add liquids to the dry ingredients, and stir to just dampen the dry ingredients. Do not overmix, as trapped air will cause "tunneling." Fold the berries into the batter. Carefully push the batter into well-greased and floured muffin tins. Do not fill more that one-third full, to discourage the berries from settling to the bottom and so causing soggy muffins. Bake in an oven preheated to 350°F for 25 minutes. Makes 8 to 12 medium-size muffins.

Watervliet, N.Y.

DESSERTS

The Trustees' Office and Guest House, Center Family,
North Union, Ohio

DESSERTS

The real skill of a cook is measured by her cake baking. – A Shaker sister.

What fragrances would have whetted our appetites if we could have visited the mammoth North Union Shaker kitchens when a dozen pungent puddings aquiver with lush spices and dark juicy molasses emerged at dinner time emerged after hours of baking in old brick ovens. Often this fragrance was mingled with that from rows of steaming berry pies or small hills of doughnuts still wreathed in the aroma of hot butter and nutmeg.

The travel journals of Shakers visiting the Valley of God's Pleasure tell how their hosts served picnic suppers in their Hemlock Grove. This was the community's recreation ground located on the bank of Doan Brook, reaching to the Lower Lake near the Mill Family village. On these occasions there emerged from Believers' great food hampers substantial dishes such as baked hash, Shaker fish and eggs, scalloped potatoes, huge loaves of freshly baked bread to be sliced on the spot and spread with tasty herb butters. There were crocks of crisp pickles and a whole arrays of juicy pies and slabs of cake as well as crullers, tarts and quantities of fresh cold milk.

In *Mary Whitcher's Shaker House-Keeper* there are recipes for Spanish creams, chocolate pudding, steamed puddings with various sauces, snow pudding with a golden sauce; baked cornstarch, apple, bread-and-butter, rice, sago and plum puddings; recipes for ambrosia and nineteen varieties of cakes and an equal assortment of cookies; for creams, gelatines, baked fruits, pan dowdy and countless cranberry dishes, for soufflés and custards besides pies, dumplings and tarts.

We read: "Food was good at the Shaker communities and the lusty appetites of the hard workers of their households, and of their many guests who often had traveled many miles, complimented the Shaker cooks."

Tin sugar shaker from Canterbury, N.H.

QUAINT COOKING TERMS: These are some terms found in very early Shaker household journals:

"Searce the sugar" referred to maple or brown sugar and meant sieve out all lumps and make fine.

"Pie coffin" was a term used to define the case of a pie shell.

"Cart an egg" mean to beat it.

ASSORTED DESSERTS

Shaker Applesauce

2 pounds dried apples
5½ cups water
11 cups Cider Concentrate
1 cup sugar (optional)
1 teaspoon cinnamon, ground
½ teaspoon nutmeg, ground
¼ teaspoon cloves, ground

Soak apples overnight in water in the refrigerator. Drain, and add cider concentrate, sugar, if used, and spices. Place in an enameled, glass or stainless steel covered saucepan and simmer 3½ hours. Do not stir. Apple slices should remain whole and float in the rich, dark syrup. Chill. Makes about 3 quarts.

Sister Ethel Peacock, Sabbathday Lake

Shaker Cider Concentrate

1 gallon fresh apple cider

In a large non-metallic pot, simmer the cider until it is reduced to about 5½ to 6 cups. Pour into a sterilized jar, cover and refrigerate until needed.

NOTE: Frozen concentrated apple juice may be substituted for the cider concentrate in any recipe.

Shaker Apple Dumplings

4 tart apples
Pastry for two 9" pie crusts (See Index)
½ cup sugar
½ cup hot maple syrup
2 tablespoons heavy cream
1 tablespoon rosewater or almond extract
½ cup hot maple syrup

Peel and core large, pleasantly sour apples, such as Granny Smith or Greening. Place them in a solution of 2 tablespoons lemon juice and 3 cups water as you peel and core them. The citric acid will keep them from turning brown. Roll pastry to ⅛" thickness and cut into 6-inch squares or squares large enough to wrap around apple. Blend sugar, cream and extract; mix well.

Place each apple in the middle of the pastry square. Fill center of each apple with the cream mixture. Bring corners of pastry square together and moisten the edges so they will cling together when pressed about the apple. Prick pastry with fork to let steam escape. Place apples in a shallow oven-proof baking dish and bake 15 minutes in a preheated hot oven (450°F). Baste with hot syrup; reduce heat to 350°F and bake another 30 minutes, basting with syrup every 15 minutes. Serve with Hard Sauce (see Index). Makes 4 individual servings.

To ¼ cup of water, add sugar and salt. Bring to the boiling point, to form a syrup. Dissolve gelatin in ¼ cup cold water and add to hot syrup. Add juices and rind and chill. Freeze in an ice cream freezer until mushy. Pack and let freeze.

Grape Juice Ice

2 cups water
1 cup sugar
⅛ teaspoon salt
1 tablespoon gelatin
2 cups grape juice
½ cup lemon juice
Grated rind of half an orange

Dessert Omelet

4 tart, medium apples
Water or cider
½ cup sugar
½ teaspoon nutmeg or apple pie spice
4 eggs, well beaten
1 tablespoon butter
Cinnamon for dusting

Cut apples in large pieces. Place into an enameled, glass or stainless steel saucepan and simmer, covered, in enough water or cider to keep them from sticking to the pan. Add more as needed. When apples are soft (about 15 to 20 minutes) pass them through a sieve or food mill. Stir in sugar and seasoning, and set aside to cool. When cool, stir in eggs to mix well and pour into a well-buttered baking dish or a preheated cast-iron skillet. Bake in a preheated moderately-slow oven (300°F) for about 20 minutes. Serve warm with Cider Sauce and a dusting of cinnamon. Serves 4 to 6.

NOTE: One to 1¼ cups of unsweetened applesauce may be substituted for the cooked, sieved apples.

Sister Lettie

MORE QUAINT COOKING TERMS: Among terms found in very early Shaker household journals were these:

"Beat with birchen twigs" was a term used in the "wooden" era of Shaker cooking when wire beaters were scarce.

"Pompoon" was used for pumpkin.

"Butter the size of a walnut" was one of the first attempts at exact measurement.

A FREQUENT DESSERT: After the North Union Shakers built their icehouse in 1874 and cut and stored their own ice, ice cream was a common dessert among them. Like their butter churns of that date, they had their freezer driven by water power in the dairy. "Good home-made ice cream for supper" is an entry found in several of the visiting elders' journals.

SHAKER DINING PHILOSOPHY: "When our meals are disturbed by anger, passion, hate or even haste we develop bodily disorders....All our meals should be eaten calmly and deliberately and as pleasantly as possible."—*The Manifesto*, November, 1880.

Rosewater Ice Cream

1½ cups milk
3 egg yolks
¾ cup sugar
⅛ teaspoon salt
1 pint heavy cream, whipped
1½ teaspoons rosewater

Scald milk over low heat. Beat egg yolks with sugar and salt until thick and lemon colored. Pour in the hot scalded milk, beating constantly. Return entire mixture to low heat and cook, very gently, until it is slightly thickened and coats a metal spoon. Remove from heat and chill thoroughly. Add rosewater and fold in the whipped cream. Place mixture in an ice cream freezer and process until frozen and thick. Remove dasher and pack. Let ripen for several hours. Makes about 4 servings.

Strawberry Shortcake

2 quarts strawberries
½ cup sugar
1 teaspoon salt
2 tablespoons sugar
2 teaspoons baking powder
1 cup cake flour
1 cup all-purpose flour
4 tablespoons butter
⅔ cup light cream
4 tablespoons soft butter
1 pint heavy cream, whipped with 4 tablespoons powdered sugar

Wash and hull berries. Place in a bowl, add the ½ cup sugar, and macerate or crush lightly. Chill until ready to use. Sift together salt, the 2 tablespoons sugar, baking powder, and both flours several times. Cut butter into the flour mixture with a pastry blender or 2 knives, scissors fashion, until mixture resembles coarse meal. Add cream, tossing quickly until dough leaves the sides of the bowl in a ball. Handle dough as little as possible. Divide into two equal parts and roll out each to ¼-inch thick circles. Spread each layer with 2 tablespoons soft butter and place on a greased and floured baking sheet, one on top of the other, buttered side up.

Bake in a preheated 425°F oven about 7 minutes, then reduce heat to 375°F and continue baking 7 to 8 minutes longer or until crust in nicely browned. When done and still slightly warm, split apart. Fill with a deep layer of crushed berries. Replace top crust and cover with remaining berries. Serve with soft whipped cream, or pour heavy cream over all. Serves 6 to 8.

Eldress Clymena Miner, North Union

ROSEWATER FLAVORING: There were very few flavoring extracts in the early days. Almost every household made its supply of rosewater which was used to flavor pies, cakes, puddings and custards. Grated orange and lemon peel were also used for this purpose. The Shakers made great quantities of rosewater, which requires double distilling, but it is available today at many food specialty stores, bakers' supply companies, or continental bake shops. Happily, rosewater is also still available from the Shakers themselves. Write The United Society of Shakers, Sabbathday Lake, Maine 04274, enclosing a self-addressed stamped envelope for a free catalogue of their culinary herbs and herbal teas. Both orange water and rosewater are favorites of European pastry chefs.

CAKES AND FROSTINGS

In a hand-written Shaker household journal, yellow with age and the buttery fingers of three generations of cooks, we read: "The real skill of a cook is measured by her cake baking; here you can use only the best of butter, eggs and flour, for cakes are so delicate in flavor and depend wholly on the perfect balance and right blending of ingredients—that any shortcoming will soon be detected....Your proportions must be right in cake mixing, therefore it is always wise to use carefully worked out rules and measure all your materials with great exactness....Again, have all your measures, materials and baking tins in readiness, for cake batter must not be left standing after leavening has been added. Above all, see that your oven is at proper heat for the kind of cake you are perfecting. The matter of proper heat is of utmost importance."

Sugar was very scarce at the western frontier in the early days, and for some years after the founding of our western Shaker communities, maple sugar, maple syrup, molasses and honey were the only sweetenings used, even in cake baking. The oldest cake recipes were all made this way: molasses fruit cake, maple sugar cake, plumped raisin cake, Shaker wafers (made with boiled molasses) and Shaker honey cake. The lack of sugar also accounts for the lack of fluffy, elaborate icings and frostings in the early days.

Later, when granulated sugar was readily obtainable, there were countless recipes for sponge, feather, marble, jelly roll and pound cakes, as well as hard, soft and old-fashioned ginger cake. Then, too, there is an almost endless array of small confections such as crumpets, crullers, sand tarts, sugar cookies, doughnuts, cup cakes, puffs, ginger nuts and jumbles.

MOTHER ANN'S BIRTHDAY CAKE: Mother Ann's birthday was on February 29, a date which occurs only in Leap Year, so it was usually celebrated March 1. At North Union the birthday cake was served at supper, following the long afternoon meeting commemorating the life of the Shakers' beloved founder, Ann Lee (1736-1784). The original recipe reads: "Cut a handful of peach twigs which are filled with sap at this season of the year. Clip the ends and bruise them and beat the cake batter with them. This will impart a delicate peach flavor to the cake."

This same cake was usually baked for the Christmas festival at North Union, when mounds of it were served at the lunch preceding the afternoon meeting. At that season the cake was flavored with rosewater.

Mother Ann's Birthday Cake

1 cup sweet butter, room
 temperature
2 teaspoons pure vanilla
1½ cups sugar
3½ cups cake flour
1 tablespoon baking powder
1 cup milk
12 egg whites
½ cup sugar
1 teaspoon salt

Cream the butter until it is fluffy and light. Add the flavoring and cream again. Cream in the sugar a little at a time. Sift flour and baking powder together, twice. Divide flour mixture into four parts and milk into three parts. Add flour to creamed mixture, alternately with milk, starting with flour and ending with flour; four parts flour with three parts milk. Beat well after each addition.

Beat egg whites until foamy, add salt and beat until soft peaks are formed. Gradually add remaining sugar, beating constantly, until a stiff, moist peaked meringue is formed. Pour the batter over the meringue and fold gently to combine. Do not beat at this stage.

Pour into three 8″ or 9″ greased and floured layer cake pans and bake in a preheated, 350°F oven for 25 minutes. Remove from pans after 5 minutes of cooling and continue cooling until cold. Fill between layers with peach jelly (see Index), and cover with any delicate icing or frosting.

Shaker Cider Cake

1 cup sweet butter
3 cups sugar
4 eggs
1½ teaspoons nutmeg
½ teaspoon salt
1 teaspoon baking soda
6 cups all-purpose flour
1 cup Cider Concentrate (see Index)

Cream butter. Cream in sugar, then eggs, one at a time until mixture is light and fluffy. Sift together all remaining dry ingredients 3 times. Divide into four parts. Add dry ingredient mixture to creamed mixture alternately with cider concentrate which has been separated into three parts; starting and ending with dry ingredients. Butter and flour two 10″ tube or Bundt pans and pour equal amounts of batter into each. Bake in a moderate (350°F) oven for 1 hour. Turn out onto a cake rack to cool. When cool, place in tightly closed containers and store in a cool place. Makes about 24 thinly sliced servings. Will keep for weeks if it lasts that long!

Union Village

Shaker Dried Apple Cake

1 cup dried apples
1 cup molasses
⅔ cup sour cream
1 cup granulated sugar
1 egg
1¼ cups all-purpose flour
2 teaspoons baking soda
1 teaspoon cinnamon
½ teaspoon cloves or allspice
½ teaspoon salt

Maple Sugar Cake

½ cup sweet butter
1½ cups brown sugar, packed
1 teaspoon maple flavoring
2 eggs
½ teaspoon salt
1 teaspoon baking soda
1 teaspoon cinnamon
½ teaspoon nutmeg
2½ cups all-purpose flour
1½ cups unsweetened applesauce
1 cup raisins, lightly floured
1 cup walnuts, hickory nuts, or
  pecans, coarsely chopped

Place dried apples in a bowl and add cold water to cover. Refrigerate overnight, or at least 6 hours. In the morning, drain, and chop finely on a cutting board. Place in a saucepan with molasses and when it begins to simmer, cook for 20 minutes. Cool. Combine cream, sugar and egg and beat until smooth. Combine remaining dry ingredients and sift together several times. Beat in liquids to dry ingredients until smooth. Stir in fruit and molasses mixture. Pour into a buttered and floured 8 1/4" by 4 1/2" loaf pan or equivalent, and bake in a preheated moderate (350°F) oven for 1 hour. This is a very tasty dessert. Dried apricots or prunes may be substituted for apples to add variety to the menu. Makes 6 servings.

Cream butter and flavoring. Gradually add sugar, a little at a time, and continue creaming until light and fluffy. Beat in eggs, one at a time, to blend thoroughly. Sift salt, soda, spices and flour together several times. Divide dry ingredients into four parts and add alternately with applesauce in three parts to creamed mixture, starting with dry ingredients and ending with dry ingrdients. Beat thoroughly to combine ingredients well. Combine raisins and nuts, and fold carefully into the creamed mixture. Lightly butter and dust with flour a 9" by 5" loaf tin or an 9" by 9" by 1½" square baking pan, and bake in a preheated moderate (350°F) oven for 1 hour, or 45 minutes if a square pan is used. Makes 6 to 8 servings.

A very old North Union recipe

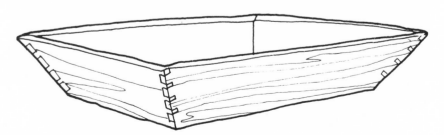

Wooden fruit tray with dovetailed corners from Canterbury, N.H., ca. 1840.

Sister Abigail's Pound Cake

1 cup sweet butter
½ teaspoon pure vanilla, almond, or
    other extract
1 cup sugar
5 eggs
2 cups sifted cake flour
¼ teaspoon mace
½ teaspoon salt

Cream butter thoroughly, add flavoring and cream again until light and fluffy. Gradually cream in the sugar, a little at a time. Cream in each egg, one at a time, beating well after each addition. Sift the flour with mace and salt, and gradually stir it into the creamed mixture. Be careful when stirring in the flour, because the eggs and the beating furnishes the leavening for this cake. Carefully pour batter into a buttered and floured 8″ by 4″ loaf pan or an 8″ tube pan. Bake for 45 minutes in a preheated moderate (350°F) oven. Makes 12 slices.

Shaker Thanksgiving Specialty

12 egg whites
1 cup sugar
1 cup sweet butter
3 cups sugar
6½ cups sifted all-purpose flour
8 teaspoons baking powder
1½ cups milk
2 quarts broken pieces of hickory,
    pecan or walnut meats

Beat egg whites until soft peaks are formed. Gradually add 1 cup sugar, a little at a time while beating, and beat until a stiff-peaked meringue is formed. Set aside. Cream butter and 3 cups sugar until light and fluffy. Combine dry ingredients and sift together several times. Divide into four parts and add alternately with milk in three parts, to the creamed mixture, starting and ending with dry ingredients. Stir briskly to combine well after each addition. (Mixture will be slightly dry.) Stir in nut meats and then gently fold in meringue. Pour into 3 buttered and floured 9″ or 10″ tube or Bundt pans and bake in a preheated moderate (350°F) oven for 45 minutes. When cool, wrap tightly or place in a sealed container, and store in a cool place (not refrigerated) for 3 to 4 weeks to ripen before cutting. To serve, slice thinly. Makes about 30 to 36 servings.

Union Village

A DELIGHTFUL EXPERIENCE: Sister Abigail's Pound Cake was always a delightful baking experience when made in our home many years ago! The careful weighing of exactly 2 pounds of sugar, 2 pounds of butter (which looked like so much good butter for just one cake!). Then the exact weighing of 2 pounds of eggs was the most thrilling part! Often larger or smaller eggs had to be substituted in order to balance the scales in true Shaker fashion. The weighing of the flour was not so exciting, but when the geranium or peach-water extract was uncorked to measure out a scant half teaspoon of one of those exotic flavorings for the great golden mass, life indeed seemed wonderful! The slow baking for three-quarters of an hour perfumed the whole house, and before the great cake was consumed, Sister Abigail had won another star for her crown.—Caroline B. Piercy

Icings

In the early days, when granulated or powdered (confectioner's) sugar was very scarce, the North Union Shakers made cake icings by boiling maple syrup and beating it into the stiffly beaten whites of eggs. Later, boiled icings and butter-cream types were used.

Although the following recipes are called "icings," they are more properly referred to as "frostings" because they are thick and fluffy, rather than thin and flowing.

Cream Icing

2 egg whites
3 cups powdered sugar, sifted
$\frac{1}{16}$ teaspoon salt
1 teaspoon heavy cream
1 teaspoon grated lemon rind

Beat egg whites until foamy. Add salt and beat until soft peaks are formed. Beat in sugar a little at a time until very stiff peaks are formed. Beat in cream and lemon rind. The recipe makes enough for the top and sides of a 9-inch two-layer cake. Cake must be completely cooled before using this icing.

Boiled Frosting

2 egg whites
$\frac{1}{8}$ teaspoon cream of tartar
$\frac{1}{3}$ cup water
1 cup granulated sugar
1 teaspoon pure vanilla

Beat egg whites with cream of tartar until soft peaks are formed. Heat water to boiling, then add granulated sugar. Cook 5 minutes without stirring. The sugar and water should be cooked to the "thread stage"; that is, until the mixture spins a two-inch thread when dropped from a fork or spoon. It is also 230°F at sea level. Pour the hot syrup over the beaten whites in a thin stream, beating constantly until cool. Beat in vanilla. This recipe makes a generous cupful, enough for the top of one 9-inch two-layer cake.

Chocolate Powdered Sugar Frosting

3½ cups powdered sugar, sifted
¼ cup heavy cream, warmed to 110°F
3 tablespoons sweet butter
1 square unsweetened chocolate
2 teaspoons pure vanilla

Stir heavy cream into powdered sugar. Melt butter with chocolate and beat into sugar-and-cream mixture until soft and creamy. Beat in vanilla. Use at once.

THANKSGIVING DAYS: It was written by one of the North Union Elders that "Every day is Thanksgiving Day at the Shaker communities, for the Believers never cease being thankful for the great bounty God bestows upon His children."

Boiled Icing

1½ cups brown sugar, packed
½ teaspoon maple flavor
⅓ cup water
2 egg whites
⅛ teaspoon salt
1 teaspoon vanilla

Boil sugar, maple flavor and water until it forms a syrup and reaches the soft ball stage (236°F). Beat egg whites until foamy. Add salt, and beat until very stiff peaks are formed. Gradually beat in hot syrup, poured in a thin stream, and then vanilla, until stiff, moist peaks are formed. This recipe makes 1 1/2 cupfuls, enough for the top and sides of an 8-inch two-layer cake. This may be spread on a warm cake.

Chocolate Icing

2 egg whites
2 cups powdered sugar, sifted
1 ounce bittersweet chocolate, grated
½ teaspoon vanilla

Beat egg whites until soft peaks are formed. Gradually beat in sugar, a little at a time, until stiff peaks are formed. Add grated chocolate, a little at a time, and beat until smooth.

NOTE: This icing has flecks of chocolate in it. If a smooth icing is desired, melt the chocolate over hot water in the top of a double boiler before beating into the whites.

COOKIES

The great cookie crock at North Union was usually filled with Sugar Cookies, for the Shakers had butter and eggs aplenty in those days. Long after the Shakers had left the Valley of God's Pleasure oldtimers who had known them fondly remembered their delicious cookies.

Shaker Ginger Chips

1 cup molasses
¼ cup sweet butter
1 teaspoon ginger
1 teaspoon baking soda
¼ teaspoon salt
½ teaspoon baking powder
2¼ cups all-purpose flour

Bring molasses to a full boil; add butter and stir well. Remove from heat. In a bowl, sift dry ingredients together and stir slowly into the hot mixture. DO NOT BEAT! Chill well. When cold, roll ⅛" thick, and cut out with a 2-inch round cutter. Place on a greased and floured baking sheet and bake in a preheated hot (400°F) oven 5 to 8 minutes. Watch carefully, for these ginger chips burn easily; in fact, anything containing molasses does. Makes about 2 dozen cookies.

If you wish a very crisp, brittle ginger cookie, try this recipe.

Sister Lettie's Sand Cakes

1 cup butter
2 cups sugar
1 teaspoon grated lemon rind
3 egg whites
3½ cups all-purpose flour
1 teaspoon salt
1 teaspoon baking powder
½ cup finely chopped nuts
½ cup powdered sugar
1 teaspoon cinnamon

Cream butter and sugar together until light and fluffy. Gradually beat in rind and egg whites until mixture is smooth and whites are incorporated. Sift flour, salt and baking powder together 3 times. Divide the flour mixture into 4 equal parts and add each part to the creamed mixture gradually, taking care to stir well after each addition. Chill mixture for about 30 to 45 minutes.

Roll out dough on a lightly floured board, to about ⅛″ thickness. Combine nuts, powdered sugar and cinnamon and sprinkle over the entire surface. Cut rolled dough into 1½″ by 1½″ squares with a pastry wheel or rounded edge of a spatula. Place each square on a lightly greased cookie sheet and bake in a preheated moderate (350°F) oven for 8 minutes. Makes about 5 dozen.

Shaker Seed Cakes

½ cup sweet butter
1½ cups sugar
3 eggs
1 teaspoon anise seed
3 cups cake flour
1 egg white, beaten slightly with 2 tablespoons water
½ cup blanched almonds

The recipe for these, from an old manuscript cook book, adds this bit of advice: "Let these cakes ripen for several days before serving. Keep in an earthen jar, well out of sight, for they are very tempting!"

Cream butter well. Cream in sugar gradually. Cream in one egg at a time, until light and fluffy. Stir in the anise seed and then, gradually, the flour. Roll to ½″ thickness on a lightly buttered cookie sheet. Cut into diamond shapes, 1½″ long, with a wavy-edged pastry wheel. Brush with diluted egg white and press whole blanched almond into the center of each diamond. Bake in a preheated, moderate (350°F) oven about 12 minutes. Makes about 2½ dozen cookies.

"SAINTS' HEARTS": Sand tarts or cakes long ago were known as "Saints' Hearts" and had their origin in the early Christian church. On saints' days they were baked in the shape of hearts. The ancient recipe found its way into the Shaker kitchens and became a favorite among the Belivers—perhaps because like Shaker food these little sand tarts were once upon a time tinctured with religious zeal.

Shaker Sugar Cookies

1 cup sweet butter
2 cups sugar
3 eggs
½ teaspoon grated lemon peel
¼ teaspoon nutmeg
¾ teaspoon cream of tartar
1 teaspoon salt
4 to 4½ cups all-purpose flour
1 cup decorative coarse sugar crystals

Cream butter and sugar. Reserve ½ egg white for brushing cookies. Add remaining eggs to creamed mixture, one at a time, creaming well after each addition. Stir in lemon peel and nutmeg. Sift remaining dry ingredients together, three times. Stir into creamed mixture a little at a time. Start with 4 cups flour and add more if necessary to form dough into a ball. Cover and chill for half an hour.

Roll out to ¼" thickness and cut with 2½-inch round cookie cutter. Place on lightly greased and floured cookie sheet and brush with egg white. Sprinkle generously with decorative coarse sugar crystals. Bake in a preheated hot (400°F) oven for 10 minutes. Makes about 3 dozen cookies. If you prefer crisper cookies, roll out dough to only ⅛" thickness, to make about 6 dozen cookies. Bake only 5 to 7 minutes.

Eldress Clymena Miner, North Union.

Shaker Sour Cream Cookies

3 eggs
1 cup sugar
1 cup sour cream
¾ teaspoon baking soda
¼ teaspoon nutmeg
3 cups cake flour

Beat eggs until frothy. Slowly beat in sugar a little at a time. Beat in sour cream. Sift dry ingredients together and stir into egg mixture. Drop by teasoonfuls onto a buttered and floured cookie sheet. Bake in a preheated hot (400°F) oven 10 to 12 minutes. Makes about 3 to 3½ dozen 1½" cookies. These wonderfully good cookies are from an old Enfield community recipe.

Sister Marguerite, Canterbury.

PIES AND PASTRY

The founders of North Union brought their pie-making skills with them from New England. After the grist mill in the Valley of God's Pleasure began grinding an ample assortment of flours and meals, the Shaker sisters showed great ingenuity in wrapping almost anything edible—from garden, herd, flock and orchard—in an endless variety of pastries. The brethren, coming in to breakfast at 6 o'clock aftrer an hour or more of milking and other heavy chores, wanted something solid and satisfying—something that would stick to the ribs, such as hash, eggs, oatmeal, stewed fruits, ample slices of coffee cake, slabs of pie and doughnuts.

In the Shaker pantries there was a constant rotation of green and dried apple pies, and when the apple bins had to be scraped in the late winter for the last few Greenings and Winesaps, delicate custards were added to stretch out this delicious fare. All summer there were berries and other lush fruits, both wild and cultivated, which the skillful sisters encased in crusty pastry. Later, cranberries, mincemeat, squash and pumpkin filled the shells. The Shakers had a veritable calendar of pies.

Pie basket, 12½" in diameter.

Suggestions for Making Pastry Successfully

1. The most important point in making a flaky pastry crust is to have the shortening well chilled. This keeps the fat particles from being absorbed by the flour. A pastry blender or two knives, scissors fashion, are best to cut in the shortening. Using the fingers to cut in shortening warms the fat which is then absorbed by the flour.
2. Overhandling or adding too much liquid results in less tender pastry.
3. When rolling the dough, place on a lightly floured board and roll from the center to the edges with short, quick strokes until the dough is almost transparent (about 1/8-inch thickness). Lift the rolling pin as it nears the edges to obtain pastry that is of even thickness.
4. Do not oil or grease baking utensils. The fat in the pastry is sufficient to prevent sticking.
5. Do not stretch the dough when placing it into the baking utensil. Abnormal shrinking will occur, causing the pie crust to fall towards the center.
6. If a pie shell is to be baked before filling, pinch or prick the bottom with a fork many times to ensure air escaping from the holes made. An uneven baked pie shell is caused by the air trapped in the bottom between the pie pan and the pastry shell.
7. Use various types of decorative edgings to dress-up the presentation of a pie. These edgings also serve to seal in the juices of most two-crust pies. Be sure to place the overhanging top crust between the bottom crust and the baking utensil to further insure the seal.
8. Do not use pastry scraps or trimmings, unless used half-and-half with fresh pastry. Mix the two gently and then use only for the bottom crust or for decorative leaves, flowers, etc.
9. A two-crust pie requires steam-escape holes to be placed either in the center or around the surface of the top crust. These holes are usually concealed as part of the decoration.

Shaker Apple Pie

4 or 5 sour apples, medium size
⅔ cup sugar
1 tablespoon cream
1 tablespoon rosewater or almond extract
Pastry for 2 nine-inch crusts
½ teaspoon rosewater or almond extract
¼ cup milk

Peel, core and slice apples into a mixing bowl and add sugar, cream and extract. Mix thoroughly to coat apples. Line the pie pan with pastry and fill with the apple mixture. Cover with the top crust and place a vent hole in the center, or slash in 3 or 4 places to allow steam to escape. Tuck the outer edges of the top crust under the bottom crust to prevent the juices from spilling over. Brush surface with extract and milk mixed together. Bake in a preheated moderate oven (350°F) for about 50 minutes.

Canterbury

Sift flour, salt and baking powder together 3 times. Cut in butter with a pastry blender or two knives, scissors-fashion, until fat particles are the size of small peas or beans. With a two-tine fork, stir in ice water, a little at a time, stirring briskly to incorporate as much air as possible. Add only enough water to form a dough that leaves the sides of the bowl in a ball and is not sticky. Form into two balls and chill slightly. Roll to ⅛" thickness on a lightly floured board. Makes two 9" pie crusts especially suited to fruit pies.

Sister Lettie's Butter Pastry

2¼ cups all-purpose flour
½ teaspoon salt
½ teaspoon baking powder
⅔ cup unsalted butter, chilled
⅓ cup to 1/2 cup ice water (variable)

Place cider concentrate in a non-metallic, or enameled or stainless steel saucepan. Add butter, sugar, syrup and salt. Simmer several minutes until butter melts. Beat a little of the hot syrup into the beaten egg yolks to heat the yolks and prevent curdling. Beat this mixture into the remaining syrup mixture to blend thoroughly. Beat egg whites until soft peaks are formed. Gradually beat in the remaining sugar and continue beating until a stiff meringue is formed. Gently fold yolk mixture into the meringue to blend. Pour into the unbaked pie shell and dust the surface with nutmeg. Bake in an oven, preheated to 425°F, for 10 minutes to set the crust. Reduce temperature to 350°F and continue baking until custard is set; about 35 minutes.

South Union

Shaker Cider Pie

½ cup Cider Concentrate (see Index)
1 tablespoon butter
½ cup brown sugar, packed
¼ cup maple syrup
1/16 teaspoon salt
2 egg yolks, slightly beaten
2 egg whites
¼ cup sugar
1 unbaked 9-inch pie shell
1/16 teaspoon nutmeg

Mix sugar with flour and flavoring extract. Sprinkle over fruit in a bowl and mix well. Pour into pastry shell, cover with top crust and pierce to allow steam to escape. Bake in a preheated moderate oven (375°F) for about 35 to 40 minutes.

Shaker Cranberry Pie

¾ cup sugar
1 tablespoon flour
1 teaspoon flavoring extract (vanilla, orange or lemon)
1 cup raisins
1 cup cranberries
Pastry for two-crust pie

Kentucky Shoo Fly Pie

¾ cup dark molasses
¾ cup boiling water
1½ cups flour
½ teaspoon baking soda
½ cup brown sugar, packed
¼ cup butter
Pastry for 1 crust

Mix molasses with hot water and blend well. Prepare crumb mixture by sifting together flour, sugar and soda. Cut in butter until the mixture resembles coarse meal. Line 9″ pie dish with pastry. Pour in third of the molasses mixture and top with third of the crumb mixture. Repeat layering process twice more, alternating layers of syrup and crumbs, ending with crumbs on top. Bake in a preheated oven (375°F) for about 35 minutes.

Shaker Lemon Pie

2 lemons
¼ cup cornstarch
¼ cup cold water
1¼ cups sugar
1¾ cups boiling water
3 egg yolks, beaten lightly
3 egg whites
2 tablespoons sugar
1½ teaspoons lemon juice
⅛ teaspoon salt
1 baked pie shell

Roll lemons on the work surface with the palms of your hands to soften. Grate yellow "zest" or rind and reserve. Squeeze out juice and reserve. In a double boiler, over hot water, mix sugar, cornstarch and cold water. Add boiling water and cook until heated thoroughly and well thickened, stirring occasionally. To egg yolks in a bowl, pour a small amount of the hot, thickened mixture and stir to blend. Pour egg mixture gradually into the remaining thickened cornstarch mixture, stirring constantly. Return to double boiler bottom to cook for 5 minutes longer, or until egg yolk begins to thicken.

Remove from heat and add lemon zest and juice. Stir until smooth. Pour into a baked pie shell and chill. Beat egg whites with salt until soft peaks are formed. Beat in lemon juice gradually, and then sugar, a little at a time, until mixture stands in stiff, moist peaks, and forms a meringue. Top lemon custard filling with meringue and bake in a very hot oven 3 to 4 minutes to brown the meringue.

Union Village

PASTRY VARIETIES: There were sundry pastries for the various foods, as this entry in the old Shaker annals suggests: "Venison and mutton must be baked in a moist, thick and lasting crust for which a rye-paste is the best. Turkey, veal and lamb should be baked in a good white flour crust, somewhat thick. Chicken, quince and mincemat, which must be eaten hot, should have the finest, shortest wheaten crust…For tarts use puff-paste made from the choicest wheaten flour and butter. This must be handled gently…."

Melt butter in a saucepan and blend in sugar. Gradually add syrup and hot half and half, and stir until sugar is well dissolved. Dissolve cornstarch in cold milk and beat into eggs with salt. Pour the hot mixture into the cold mixture, beating constantly to prevent curdling. Pour mixture into an unbaked pie shell and sprinkle with nutmeg. Bake in a preheated moderate oven (350°F) until custard filling is set, about 25 to 30 minutes.

Simmer ground beef in a skillet with ½ cup cider, until all red coloring is gone. Blend with remaining ingredients and place in a large crock to ripen. The alcoholic content of the brandy and wine will keep the mixture from spoiling while it is ripening. Keep sealed for at least 1 month in the refrigerator before using in pies. Bake between two 9″ crusts in a preheated oven (350°F) for about 50 minutes. Serve warm or hot.

Enfield

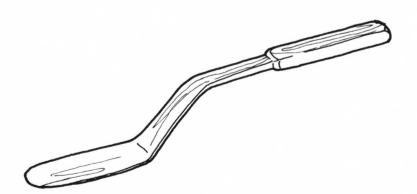

STOCKPILING MINCE PIES: Mince pies were baked by the dozen by the Shakers and stored in barrels in some cold place where they froze and kept perfectly until used, when they were thawed out, then heated and eaten hot with lemon sauce.

Sister Lettie's Maple Pie

2 tablespoons butter
1 cup brown sugar, packed
½ cup pure maple syrup
¾ cup half-and-half, hot
3 eggs
2 tablespoons cornstarch
2 tablespoons cold milk
½ teaspoon salt
Pastry for one crust
⅛ teaspoon nutmeg

Mincemeat for Pies

3½ pounds ground beef, not too lean
½ cup cider
2 pounds seedless raisins
2 pounds currants
2 pounds granulated sugar
2 pounds dark brown sugar, packed
½ pound diced candied citron
¼ pound diced candied fruit
6 cups sour apples, chopped
1 tablespoon cinnamon
1 teaspoon nutmeg
1 teaspoon allspice
½ teaspoon salt
Rind and juice of 2 lemons
1 cup Cider Concentrate (see Index)
  or medium dry white wine
½ cup brandy

Hand-carved maple spatula, 12¼″ long, from Sabbathday Lake.

Sister Lottie's Nut Crust

⅔ cup graham cracker crumbs
⅔ cup walnut meats, finely chopped
2 tablespoons melted butter
1 egg white, unbeaten

Mix crumbs and nuts. Stir in the melted butter and the unbeaten egg white. Press into the bottom and sides of a 9″ pie plate. Bake in a preheated moderate oven (350°F) for 8 to 10 minutes. Cool thoroughly before using. Fill with ice cream, custard or cream filling.

Ohio Lemon Pie

2 lemons
2 cups sugar
Pastry for 2 crusts
4 eggs

This is yet another very old lemon pie recipe which the early Ohio Shakers fashioned frequently. "Slice two lemons as thin as paper, rind and all. Place them in a bowl (it states 'yellow bowl') and pour over them 2 cups of sugar. Mix well and let stand for 2 hours or better. Then go about making your best pastry for 2 crusts. Line a pie dish with same. Beat 4 eggs together and pour over lemons. Fill unbaked pie shell with this and add top crust with small vents cut to let out steam. Place in a hot oven [at 450°F] for 15 minutes and then cut down heat and bake until a silver knife inserted into custard comes out clean."

Pastry

2¼ cups all-purpose flour
1/½ teaspoon salt
⅔ cup chilled shortening
⅓ cup ice water

Sift flour with salt into mixing bowl. Cut in the shortening with a pastry blender, or with 2 knives, scissors fashion, until the fat particles are the size of small peas or beans. With a two-tine fork stir water into the flour mixture gradually, a little at a time, until the mixture leaves the sides of the bowl in a ball. Refrain from handling dough, which would toughen the pastry. Form into 2 balls and chill until ready to use. Roll out each ball on a lightly floured board to about ⅛″ thickness. Makes two 9″ pie crusts.

North Union

A North Union Household Hint: "For flakier pie crust, beat the lard until it is light and fluffy before using." Today we know that the air incorporated into the fat by whipping helps produce a flakier pie crust.

Pastry Directions from Long Ago: The butter- and time-stained records of North Union's Shaker cooks state: "To a gallon of flour take a pound of the best butter boiled in a little pure water and make up the paste as quickly and lightly as possible...." Or: "Take a gallon of wheat flour, a pound of sugar, half a pound of butter, a pinch of saffron (it gives it a lush look); work this up with three eggs beasten to a froth, with cinnamon and a cup of rosewater."

Combine rhubarb with sugar and flour, and turn into unbaked pie shell.
Dot well with butter. Cover with top crust and cut steam vent hole in
center or slits over the surface to let steam escape. Bake in a preheated hot
oven (400°F) for 10 minutes, the reduce heat to 375°F and continue baking
until well browned, about 30 minutes. If rhubarb is unavailable, substitute
fresh cranberries for the rhubarb.

Mix all ingredients together, except pie shell. Blend thoroughly. Pour into
unbaked pie shell and bake in an oven, preheated to 425°F, for 10 minutes
to set crust. Reduce heat to 325°F and continue baking until a knife blade
inserted at the center comes out clean, about 45 minutes longer.

Amelia's Shaker Recipes

Prepare butter pastry and roll out to ⅛-inch thickness. Line a DEEP pie
dish with pastry, being careful to keep pastry unbroken. Cream butter until
light and fluffy. Spread half of the butter over the pastry. Sprinkle with
half of the sugar. Repeat with remaining butter and sugar. Sprinkle surface
with flour. Add flavoring to cream and pour over the mixture in the pie
dish. Dust the surface with nutmeg. Bake in a preheated oven (450°F) for
10 minutes. Reduce heat to 350°F and bake until a knife blade inserted at
the center comes out clean, approximately 25 minutes.

South Union

SHAKER PIE VOCABULARY: From New England the Shaker sisters brought
with them the terms "trap," "coffin," "grated" and "tart pie." The trap was a
deep-dish pie often of meat, fowl or fruit. When this trap was covered with a
top crust it was called a coffin, for it was baked in a loaf pan and resembled a
coffer or coffin. When the tart was latticed over with narrow strips of pastry
it was termed a grated pie, while the shallow, open fruit pie was called a tart.

Pieplant (Rhubarb) Pie

2 cups rhubarb, cut into one-inch
   pieces
1½ cups brown sugar
1 tablespoon flour
3 tablespoons butter
Pastry for two crusts

Pumpkin Pie

1 cup pumpkin, cooked and strained
⅔ cup brown sugar, packed
½ teaspoon ginger
½ teaspoon cinnamon
3 eggs
2 cups light cream or evaporated milk
½ teaspoon salt
1 unbaked 9″ pie shell

Sister Lizzie's Sugar Pie

1 recipe Sister Lettie's
   Butter Pastry
½ cup soft butter
1 cup brown sugar
¼ cup sifted flour
2 cups heavy cream
½ teaspoon vanilla, rosewater or
   almond extract
⅛ teaspoon nutmeg

PUDDINGS

Puddings are thick, soft or creamy desserts that can be made in a variety of ways, and they were favorite way to conclude a meal at North Union. Sister Lettie had some firm advice for her fellow workers in the kitchen who might want to prepare boiled puddings: "The outside of some boiled pudding tastes disagreeable—sort of musty. This is due to the pudding cloth not being kept for puddings only! Or perhaps the cloth has not been boiled out or washed properly after each using....Each time before using, your pudding cloth should be dipped in boiling water, squeezed out dry and well dusted with flour. If bread crumbs are used in the pudding, the bag must be tied loosely; if batter is used, tie bag very tightly. The pudding pot must be boiling very hard when the pudding is plunged in. Have a pot of cold water in readiness to dip boiling pudding into immediately as it comes from the boiling, otherwise it will adhere to cloth."

Busy Day Dessert

6 large, tart apples
1 cup water
1 cup sour cream
¼ teaspoon baking soda
3 tablespoons sugar
¼ teaspoon nutmeg
3 tablespoons melted sweet butter
1 recipe drop biscuits

Peel core and quarter apples. Place water and apples into a 3-quart casserole. Mix together cream, soda, sugar and nutmeg and blend well. Pour cream mixture over apples. Drop biscuit dough by spoonfuls over entire surface. Cover tightly and bake in a preheated moderate (325°F) oven 50 minutes. Uncover and raise heat to 375°F. Brush surface with melted butter and continue baking 10 minutes longer. Spoon out into serving dishes, inverting spoon so apples are on the top of the dumplings. Top with hard sauce or pudding sauce (see Index). Serves 8 generously.

THE SHAKER ORDER OF CHRISTMAS: "As the signal by which all the true followers of the Christ are known, is unfeigned and unalloyed love to each other, the order of God requires that on Christmas day Believers should make perfect reconciliation, one with an other; and leave all grudges, hard feelings, and disaffection one towards an other, eternally behind on this day; and to forgive as we would be forgiven; and nothing which is this day settled, or which has been previous to this, may hereafter be brought forward against an other."—The Millenial Laws, 1840s.

Christmas Bread Pudding

"Butter an ample baking dish. Cover the bottom with fairly thick slices of bread, generously buttered. Then add a goodly layer of currants, also one of shredded citron, of candied orange peel and candied lemon peel, if you have it. Then spread with a layer of strawberry jam, not too thin, for remember it is Christmas! Then repeat these layers until the dish is two-thirds filled. Then pour over this an unboiled custard made of plenty of eggs and rich milk; remember it is Christmas! Let stand for at least two hours. Then add a pretty fluting of your best pastry around the very edge of the dish; this touch is not necessary but it adds much to the gayety [sic] of the dish. Now bake until the crust is well set and the top is a rich and appetizing golden brown. Eat it with much relish, for remember it is Christmas!"

Shaker Christmas (Plum) Pudding

2 pounds raisins
2 cups wine or cider
1 pound suet, chopped fine or 1 cup butter and 1 cup ground beef
2 cups milk
½ cup maple syrup
12 egg yolks
7½ cups all-purpose flour
1½ teaspoons salt
1 teaspoon mace
1 tablespoon cinnamon
1 tablespoon ginger
12 egg whites

Heat wine or cider to simmering, in an enameled, glass or stainless steel saucepan. Place raisins in a bowl and pour in hot wine or cider. Cover, and let stand at least 2 hours, then refrigerate until cold. Beat suet or butter until soft and creamy, and add beef, if used. Beat egg yolks and add to milk and maple syrup. Drain raisins well and reserve liquid. Mix all remaining ingredients except egg whites and combine with wine or cider in which the raisins were plumped. Beat egg whites until stiff and fold into batter.

Pack mixture in a buttered 8-cup pudding basin or 2 empty one-pound coffee cans. Be sure to tie buttered brown paper over the top of each container, or use a covered pudding mold. Place containers on a rack in a large pot, taking care that simmering water not touch the pudding containers. Cover and steam for about 3 hours. Check water level each hour and replace if necessary. (The original pudding recipe states: "Pour into a strong pudding bag which has been wet and well dusted with flour. Do not tie too tightly, for remember the pudding will swell. Plunge into a boiling pot and boil for 3 hours.") Eat while very hot with Hard Sauce or Soft Sauce (see Index). Serves 12.

Sister Amelia, North Union

Shaker Ginger Fluff

½ cup sweet butter
½ cup sugar
2 eggs
½ cup molasses
2¼ cups all-purpose flour
1½ teaspoons baking soda
½ teaspoon salt
1½ teaspoons ginger
½ cup sour cream

Cream butter and sugar, until light and fluffy. Beat in eggs, one at a time. Stir in molasses. Sift flour, soda, salt and ginger together 3 times. Divide into four parts. Alternately add to creamed mixture with three parts sour cream, starting and ending with flour. Do not beat. Pour into a buttered pudding mold, buttered deep 9-inch cake pan, or buttered 3-quart casserole, and bake in a preheated moderate (350°F) oven for 45 minutes. Serve very hot with Lemon Sauce (see Index). Serves 8 generously.

Eldress Clymena Miner, North Union

Shaker Indian Pudding

¾ cup cornmeal
1 cup dark molasses
1 teaspoon salt
4 cups hot scalded milk
¼ teaspoon ginger
¼ teaspoon nutmeg
1 tablespoon butter
2 cups cold milk

Butter a heavy earthenware or crockery covered casserole. Put in cornmeal, molasses and salt. Add the scalded milk, cover and let stand 2 hours before refrigerating at least 8 hours or overnight. The next morning add ginger, nutmeg, butter and a cup of the cold milk and stir well. Bake uncovered, in a very slow preheated oven (250°F) until a crust forms on top. Stir thoroughly and add the other cup of cold milk. Bake slowly for 4 more hours. Stir several times while baking. When a good crust has formed, cover the pot and remove from oven. Let stand to cool slightly. Serve with cream or hard sauce. Serves 6.

NOTE: Regular grits may be substituted for the cornmeal.

Union Village

A PIONEER DESSERT: The original recipe for Shaker Indian Pudding dates back to the days when the Shaker sisters still used the old brick ovens. The directions read: "Bake from eight in the morning till four in the afternoon. This is a very tasty and favorite dish." Appone was a favorite dessert dish among the Western Reserve pioneers and consequently was often served at North Union. It was an Indian dish consisting of cornmeal, maple syrup and crushed fruit (usually wild), or berries, and baked slowly in a pot. It was usually served with butter.

SERVING IN QUANTITY: Shaker desserts were usually prepared for eight persons, for the serving at table was done in units of eight. The typical dessert recipe in this book which serves four, for example, is just half the original recipe. Young sisters were assigned to the task of preparing the desserts. For a full-sized Shaker family of 100 persons, it was necessary for them to prepare twenty-four such recipes for a single dinner.

When company arrives unexpectedly, this is a good dish to make quickly.

Combine crumbs and fat. Stir in currants, ginger and lemon rind. Beat egg yolks, whites and sugar together until frothy, and add to crumb mixture. Blend well and shape into balls the size of golf balls. Roll in flour and drop into boiling water (about 4 inches deep) or cider. They will rise to the top when done, about 20 minutes. Serve very hot with wine or cider pudding sauce. Serves 8.

South Union

Rub fuzz from 6 large, ripe quinces; pare and quarter them. Grate quinces to a pulp. Add ½ cup sugar and cream and mix well. Add rosewater or extract and beaten egg yolks. Beat whites until soft peaks are formed. Gradually beat in remaining ½ cup sugar and beat until stiff peaks are formed. Fold into the yolk mixture. Turn into a well-buttered baking dish and bake in a preheated 350°F oven for 45 minutes. Serve immediately. Serves four generously.

North Union

Scald milk; add sugar and salt. Mix cornstrarch and cold milk and stir into hot milk. Simmer gently over low heat until mixture thickens. Beat egg with flavoring and whisk into hot mixture. Return to heat for about 2 minutes, stirring constantly to heat mixture and thicken. Pour into a 4-cup mold and chill until set. Wash, pick over and hull strawberries. Crush them with a fork and add sugar. Chill. Unmold dessert onto a serving dish and top with strawberries. Red raspberries or loganberries may be substituted for strawberries. Makes 6 servings.

Pudding in Haste (Fruit Dumplings)

½ cup finely chopped suet or 1/2 cup butter, chilled and cut into bits
2 cups crumbled dried bread or cake crumbs
1 cup currants or raisins
½ teaspoon ginger
Grated rind of 1 lemon
6 egg yolks plus 2 whites
½ cup sugar
1 cup all-purpose flour
Boiling water or cider

Sister Amelia's Quince Pudding

6 large quinces OR 6 unripened peaches and 2 tablespoons flour
1 cup sugar
1 cup heavy cream
¼ cup rosewater or almond extract
6 egg yolks, lightly beaten
6 egg whites, stiffly beaten

Sister Abigail's Strawberry Flummery

2¼ cups milk
2 tablespoons sugar
¼ teaspoon salt
⅓ cup cornstarch
¾ cup milk, cold
1 beaten egg
½ teaspoon rosewater or vanilla
1 quart fresh strawberries
4 tablespoons sugar

SWEETMEATS

The Center Family Blacksmith Shop,
North Union, Ohio

SWEETMEATS

Be not angry or sour at the table; whatever may happen put on a cheerful mien, for good humor makes one dish a feast. – Gentle Manners.

Like other people, the Shakers enjoyed sweets, or "sweetmeats." In the early years, refined sugar was scarce and honey was a prized commodity. When the Shaker honey supply was low, they would spread some on a heated stone; almost immediately the bees would scent the fragrance and buzz about the bait. A boy, fleet of foot, would be hiding nearby. He would follow the bees to their lair and extract the needed sweet from the bee-tree.

Later, North Union erected a bee-house and cultivated bees. By a wonderful coincidence, the beekeeper's name was Honey—Brother Riley Honey. Said to be the first white child born on the Western Reserve, Brother Honey was one of the founders of North Union. He grew up to wield an ax, erect a cabin, boil down sugar water, catch coons and find wild honey better than almost anyone. After a lifetime of loyal service to the Shaker community, this pioneer brother became deaf and could no longer serve his community as trustee. The community set up the bee-house and for over a decade Brother Honey carried on a flourishing trade.

Of course, the maple tree was also a source of sweetness for the Shakers, and some societies the maple syrup industry was a lucrative source of income, with maple products being advertised in the newspapers the year around.

Some of the old recipes which follow require roots and herbs which, if not readily available through your usual markets, may be ordered from purveyors of "natural" foods and herbs. Be sure the products are fresh and not dried.

Maple sugar bucket from North Union.

HERB-GATHERING IN THE VALLEY OF GOD'S PLEASURE: Unlike some other societies, herbs did not constitute a major industry at North Union. Nevertheless, the Shakers there did raise sufficient herbs for their own medicinal, flavoring and other domestic needs. Their household accounts tell how the sisters "went agathering berry-tea, penny royal and catnip for teas; poke berries for ink and sundry roots and herbs for poultices and steeps."

Maple Creams

3 cups brown sugar
1 cup cream
1½ teaspoon maple flavoring
1 cup chopped pecans or walnuts

In a saucepan, cook sugar and cream to the soft ball stage (236°F) or until a soft ball is formed when dropped into cold water. Remove from heat. Beat until very creamy and candy has cooled somewhat. Add maple flavoring. Butter a large platter and sprinkle with nuts. Pour candy over nuts and let cool. Cut into squares and store covered, in a cool, dry place.

VARIATION: These candies may be dipped into melted semi-sweet chocolate to coat. Let drain on a cooling rack over wax paper.

Shaker Mints

2 cups sugar
½ cup white corn syrup
½ cup water
1 egg white
3 drops oil of peppermint
3 drops green food coloring

In a saucepan, combine sugar, corn syrup and water and cook to the hard ball stage (260°F) or until mixture forms a hard ball when dropped in cold water. While mixture is still hot, beat egg white until stiff peaks are formed. Gradually pour the hot syrup into the egg white, in a thin stream, beating constantly until smooth and creamy. Beat in flavoring and coloring, and using a buttered rubber scraper, quickly drop by small spoonfuls onto wax paper to complete cooling and setting. If mixture stiffens too much to drop easily, place in the top part of a double boiler, over hot water to soften slightly. When cooled, store in a cool dry place.

Shaker Molasses Taffy

1 cup molasses
1 cup sugar
1 cup light cream
2 tablespoons butter
1 teaspoon soda
1 cup chopped walnuts or pecans

Cook molasses, sugar and cream to the hard ball stage (260°F) or until a ball is formed when dropped in cold water. Remove from heat and add butter, soda and nuts. Pour onto a buttered platter and let cool until the edges begin to crinkle. Follow general instructions for pulling taffy.

North Union

SHAKER SUGAR-MAKING: Near Mt. Lebanon in the 1860s was a grove of nearly 1,000 maple trees, from which a bountiful harvest was collected each year, according to Sister Marcia. The sap was boiled in large kettles in the sugar camp, located on the hillside about two miles from the Shaker village. Most of the harvest was intended for sale, but Sister Marcia Bullard wrote that "when all the sale sugar was finished, the Sisters made candy for the family; each member being allowed a pound—plain, flavored or mixed to suit their fancy. The flavors were wintergreen, mint, clove, cinnamon or horehound."

Rose Haw Preserves

1 cup sugar
1 cup water
½ teaspoon rosewater or almond
    extract
2 cups rose haws (rose hips)
½ cup seedless raisins

The rose haw, or fruit of the briar rose, forms in the Fall after the bloom has gone and is much like the cranberry in appearance.

Cook sugar and water until it is reduced to 1 cup. Clip the blossom end, and with a very sharp knife remove seeds. Stuff with several raisins. Simmer gently, about 20 minutes in syrup. Stir in flavoring and pour immediately into hot, sterilized small glass containers, and seal. This rare preserve is truly an unforgettable confection.

Amelia's Shaker Recipes

Rose Petal Sweetmeat

4 cups freshly plucked rose petals
1 quart water
3½ cups sugar
¼ cup honey
1 teaspoon lemon juice
Few drops pink food coloring

Cut off hard base of the rose petals and wash thoroughly. Pack into cups and measure. Place rose petals and water in an enameled, glass or stainless steel saucepan. Simmer 10 minutes. Drain liquid and reserve 1 cup. Replace this liquid, sugar and honey in the saucepan, and cook until it threads from the spoon (230°F). Add lemon juice and simmer until petals are transparent. Color, stirring very gently, and pour into hot, sterilized jelly glasses immediately. Seal. Makes about 1 quart.

NOT JUST FOR BEAUTY: Roses grew in the Valley of God's Pleasure, as they did at other Shaker societies, but they were intended for practical uses rather than ornamentation. Of the rose, Sister Marcia of Mt. Lebanon once wrote, "It was not intended to please us by its color or its odor; its mission was to be made into rosewater, and if we thought of it in any other way we were making an idol of it and thereby imperiling our souls....The rosewater was sold, of course, and was used in the community to flavor apple pies. It was also kept in store at the infirmary, and although in those days no sick person was allowed to have a fresh flower to cheer him, he was welcome to to a liberal supply of rosewater with which to bathe his aching head."

Taffy

1 cup sugar
½ cup honey
⅛ teaspoon salt
1 tablespoon butter

Cook all ingredients together to the hard ball stage (260°F) or until a ball is formed when dropped into cold water. Pour onto a buttered platter and let cool until the edges begin to crinkle. Follow general instructions for pulling taffy.

North Union

GENERAL INSTRUCTIONS FOR PULLING TAFFY: Butter hands lightly. Pick up a portion of the taffy, as much as can be easily handled. Pull candy out to a length that can be managed without strands falling. Fold candy back upon itself and pull out. Continue process of pulling and folding until taffy is firm, light-colored and porous. Dip sharp scissors into boiing water and snip off pieces of candy onto wax paper. Let remain until cool. Wrap individually with wax paper or dredge in a mixture of 1 cup powdered sugar and ½ cup cornstarch to prevent sticking.

BEVERAGES

The Center Family Wash House,
North Union, Ohio

BEVERAGES

Only the best of spring water should be used in making beverages. Set beverages in the spring-house or hang in well for several hours before using. – Sister Lisset.

The subject of Shaker beverages is an important one, for the Believers were pioneers in the temperance movement in this country. In the early days, especially along the frontier, almost everyone washed down his meals and slaked his thirst with alcoholic drinks, ranging from cider, beer and ale to rum and whiskies.

The salt-meat diet of the day, the loneliness of living in rural areas, and the difficulty of shipping bulky grains and fruits that had not been reduced to liquids all helped make spirits attractive. So did the scarcity of safe drinking water and milk.

And so young people, farmers, hired hands, the teacher and the preacher all were apt to quench their thirst with strong drink. At every husking bee, barn raising and social event "the little brown jug" made its merry rounds. In fact, the person who didn't drink liquor at all was looked upon with suspicion and considered anti-social.

Until the Shakers had ample herds, cider was their staple beverage. And what cider! Shaker cider was famous throughout the young nation. But in 1828 the central ministry of the Shakers at New Lebanon, New York, issued an edict prohibiting the use of all alcoholic beverages throughout Shaker-dom: "Hereafter beer, cider, wines and all ardent liquors are banned on all occasions; at house-raisings, husking-bees, harvestings and all other such gatherings...." The far-famed Shaker cider was banished to the vinegar barrel, to be used in salads, sauces and pickles, or boiled down and bottled for sauces on steam puddings, or in making mincemeat or for "apple-sass."

In 1837 another edict was sent forth from New Lebanon prohibiting in all Shaker communities the use of coffee and teas, meat and tobacco except by members over sixty years of age. It was reported that "this restriction brought about a tremendous spiritual awakening among the Believers, for they learned that temperance meant curbing all carnal appetites and that they must rely for their strength and inspiration upon God rather than upon some stimulant."

Nest of oval boxes, with distinctive finger laps which permit the joints to breath and avoid warping.

Shaker Chocolate

2 ounces (squares) unsweetened
   chocolate
½ cup sugar
1 teaspoon cornstarch
⅛ teaspoon salt
2 cups boiling water
3 cups scalded milk
1 teaspoon pure vanilla extract

Melt chocolate in the top of a double boiler over boiling water. In a bowl, mix cornstarch, sugar and salt and add boiling water; mix thoroughly. Add to melted chocolate, and remove double boiler top to rangetop. Bring to a boil and boil for 1 minute. Add hot, scalded milk gradually while beating mixture with hand mixer or wire whisk. Beat in vanilla. Top with sweetened, whipped cream if desired. Serve in warmed mugs. Makes 5 to 6 mugs.

Sister Abigail, North Union

Shaker Mulled Cider

3 quarts cider
1 teaspoon whole cloves
½ teaspoon ground nutmeg
1 stick cinnamon
½ cup brown sugar

Put all ingredients in an enameled or glass pot and simmer for five minutes. Strain and serve very hot in warmed noggins (goblets). Serves 12 to 15 mugs.

Amelia's Shaker Recipes

Shaker Apple Dulcet

24-ounce jar apple jelly
4 cups boiling water
2 quarts fresh, unprocessed cider
8 to 10 sprigs fresh mint
½ teaspoon ground nutmeg
6 egg whites, room temperature
⅓ cup powdered sugar

Beat eggs whites until soft peaks are formed when the beater is lifted. Gradually add sugar while still beating, until stiff peaks form an egg white meringue that is still moist. Set aside. Whip the jelly to a froth by gradually beating in the boiling water. Let cool and add cider. Dust with nutmeg. Refrigerate until chilled thoroughly. Pour into tall mugs or iced-tea glasses and top generously with the meringue. Insert a sprig of mint into each mug or glass before serving. Makes 8 to 10 servings.

South Union

THE BEST CIDER: Cider was made by selecting perfect apples (a late fall apple was preferred). "Place them on the grass on the north or shady side of the grain barn to mellow. When at thirty feet distance you catch the fragrant apple aroma, they are ready for the press," the rule states. Probably what made Shaker cider outstanding was the fact that the Shakers never dumped culls or tainted apples into their presses.

"THE FRUITFUL YEAR": The Shakers were very successful orchardists. At North Union they planted two good-sized orchards at each of their three villages. In 1840 the yield of fruit was so great that the year went down in their records as "The Fruitful Year." Six hundred barrels of apples were harvested that season in this small community.

Shaker Eggnog

6 egg yolks
6 egg whites
6 tablespoons sugar
½ cup apple brandy or applejack
2 cups heavy cream
1½ quarts milk
½ teaspoon ground nutmeg

Heat 4 tablespoons of the sugar in a skillet until it is very warm, but has not browned nor melted. Gradually beat into the egg yolks until yolks are thick and lemon colored. Beat in brandy. Beat egg whites until soft peaks are formed and gradually add the remaining 2 tablespoons sugar, continuing to beat until stiff, moist peaks are formed when the beater is lifted. Pour the cream, then the milk into the beaten yolks gradually, folding gently as you pour.

Pour into tall glasses and top with the beaten egg white meringue. Dust the top of each serving with nutmeg. This is a very nourishing dish for the sick or aged, and may be served hot, if desired. Makes 6 to 8 tall glasses or 8 to 10 mugs.

South Union

Shaker Gingerade

4 ounces FRESH ginger root
4 lemons, cut in half lengthwise
2 quarts boiling water
2 cups lemon juice
Simple syrup to taste

Shred the ginger root on the shredding plate of a 4-sided grater. Add the lemons, cut into paper-thin slices. Pour the boiling water over this mixture and let stand, covered, for 5 minutes. Strain and chill. Add the lemon juice and sweeten with simple syrup to taste. Pour over shaved, chipped or crushed ice in tall glasses. In hot weather, sprigs of mint inserted in glasses add interest to this beverage. Makes about 8 tall iced-tea glasses.

Union Village

THE CLEANLINESS OF BARNS: Milk, which today is considered healthful food, was looked upon with suspicion in the early 1800s. The cows which supplied the milk for the cities in those days were kept in dark, crowded pens, and seldom had any exercise or sunlight. They often were not fed green food but were given a diet of the fermented grain used to produce alcohol in the nearby distillery. As a result, the milk was far less healthful than it could have been.

By contrast, the Shaker herds presented a wholly different picture. The Believers imported fine cattle. Their barns and stables were models of cleanliness, and the animals were kindly treated. Often the walls were ceiled and kept spotless. In fair weather the sisters did the milking. The Shakers had a marked influence on improving dairy conditions in our young land and in furnishing good wholesome milk to the public. The cattle barns at Hancock and at New Lebanon were model barns in their day.

Shaker Haying Water or Switchel

1 quart hot water
2 cups sugar, or 1½ cups pure maple
   syrup
1 cup molasses
1 teaspoon ground ginger
3 quarts ice water

In a large jug, mix together all ingredients except ice water. Cool. Add ice water and chill thoroughly. Makes a generous gallon, enough for 14 to 16 tall iced-tea glasses.

Certain Shaker beverages were spiced with pepper or ginger, for the brethren working in the fields of the heat of summer considered them very refreshing. Modern palates might not agree; our cola drinks, however, might have seemed as strange to the Shakers.

Shaker Herbade

1 tablespoon grated lemon rind
½ cup chopped mint, fresh sorrell or
   other aromatic herb
½ cup lemon juice
½ cup hot simple syrup
¼ cup orange juice
4 quarts ginger ale or Shaker
   gingerade

Combine the first 4 ingredients and let stand 1 hour. Add the remaining ingredients and stir well. Pour over crushed ice in tall glasses. Garnish each with sprig of herb. Makes 12 tall iced-tea glasses.

FOR QUENCHING THIRSTS: In haying season, or when the brethren were working on the public roads (where they spent double the allotted time working out the road tax, so as to be exempt from military service) gallons of thirst-quenching Switchel were carried to them at regular intervals. Before the Shakers at North Union had icehouses, they made up gallons of Switchel daily during the hot weather, and in order to cool it, either kept it in their springhouses or hung the great jugs filled with the beverage down in the wells. Enormous quantities of this drink were consumed each summer by the brethren working in the shops and fields as well.

THE VALUE OF THE LEMON: The Shakers greatly appreciated the lemon. They raised almost all their own food, but considered lemons such a necessary part of their diet that they were said to be the first food ever purchased by North Union. Lemons were used in pies, custards, sauces and beverages.

An article in the April, 1881, issue of *The Manifesto* published by the Shakers not only called lemonade "one of the healthiest and most refreshing drinks of all drinks," but also recommended lemons as an excellent cleansing agent on fingernails, as a rinse for hair when shampooing, and as a mouth wash.

Shaker-Style Lemonade

6 lemons
1 cup sugar
1 cup boiling water
8 cups ice water

Roll the lemons on a cutting board with the palm of your hand until the firmness softens. Cut each in half and squeeze out juice. Do not discard rinds. Strain out pulp and seeds. Add the sugar and ice water. Pour the boiling water over the lemon rinds and let stand until cold. (The hot water extracts the oil from the rinds and adds greatly to the flavor.) Add to the juice mixture and combine well.

Place a small amount of ice into each of 8 chilled mugs. Pour in chilled lemonade. Very refreshing for the sick and aged.

Sister Amelia, North Union

Shaker Mint Cup

2 cups tender fresh mint leaves, cut fine
2 cups sugar
2 cups water
⅛ teaspoon salt
2 quarts ginger ale or Shaker Gingerade

Make a simple syrup by boiling the water and sugar 3 minutes. Add salt (to help draw out the mint flavor from the leaves). Pour boiling syrup over leaves and let stand until cool. Strain, and discard the leaves. Chill thoroughly. Add ginger ale or Gingerade. Serve very cold, in tall glasses over crushed ice. Modern users of this recipe may prefer to take what has been prepared thus far and put it in a blender with ice and 2 jiggers of green crème de menthe. Blend to a frappé. Garnish each glass with a sprig of fresh mint. Makes 8 to 10 tall iced-tea glasses.

Sister Mary Gass, Whitewater Shakers

Cool Pleasures: During warm weather the Shakers could enjoy a variety of cold (though non-alcoholic) drinks. They were able to store food and chill their summer drinks with ice carefully stored the winter before. Indeed, the North Union Shakers were the first settlers in the area to erect icehouses and fill them with ice from their large lakes. Of these buildings it was written: "The double walls of the icehouse were packed with sawdust from their mill and the three-ply roof was filled with the same protection from the summer heat. The buildings were windowless. The stone floor was covered with hay and then with a layer of sawdust."

Shaker Fruit Shrub

2 quarts red raspberries or other
   berries in season
1 cup lemon juice
1½ cups sugar
2 quarts water

Make a thin syrup by boiling the water and sugar for 3 minutes. Crush berries and pour hot syrup over fruit. Let stand until cool, and strain. Add lemon juice and pour over a little crushed ice. This is a delightful and refreshing drink. Makes 6 to 8 tall iced-tea glasses.

Sister Lisset, North Union

Strawberry Cup

2¼ quarts freshly picked strawberries
¼ cup cider vinegar
4 cups sugar

Line a strainer with 8 layers of cheesecloth, or use a jelly bag. Wash, hull and crush the berries. Reserve four large, ripe berries for garnish. Place in a stainless steel bowl or enameled pot or pan and cover with vinegar. Let stand four days in a cool place. Strain the mixture through the cheesecloth and add the sugar. Bring to a boil and simmer for 5 minutes. Pour over chipped or crushed ice in tall iced-tea glasses, and garnish with the reserved berries. Makes one quart; enough for 4 to 6 tall glasses.

Amelia's Shaker Recipes

Simple Syrup

3 cups sugar
2 cups boiling water
1/16 teaspoon cream of tartar

Place all ingredients together in a quart jar and stir well to dissolve the sugar. Refrigerate until needed.

CRAFTSMANSHIP IN ICE: An old resident who as a young man helped the Shakers cut ice on the lakes of what is now the Cleveland metropark system used to tell how carefully the Shakers scraped all the snow from the surface before marking it into five-foot squares. "They saw to it that those markings were exactly straight and even," he recalled. "They never tolerated sloppy work of any kind.

"Very special curved saws carved the great cakes of ice from the frozen lakes. When a thaw or snowstorm threatened the ice crop, we often worked late into the night harvesting what we could. When the icehouse was filled, we sealed her up until summer. If the weather was really cold, our beards would hang with icicles!"

PRESERVES, JAMS, JELLIES

The East Family Dwelling House,
North Union, Ohio

PRESERVES, JAMS, JELLIES

*We sat down to a most satisfactory supper at North Union, every morsel of which
we enjoyed. – A visiting elder.*

Each of the three Shaker familes at North Union—the Mill (or North)
Family, the Center Family, and the Gathering (or East) Family—had its own
large orchards and gardens. The orchards yielded plums, peaches, pears,
cherries and tart quinces, but apples most of all: the early varieties, such as
Red Astrachan, Rambo, Grimes Golden and Yellow Hawley; the fall eating
varieties, such as Striped Northern Spy, La Belle Fameuse (Snow Apple),
Peck's Pleasant, and Maiden's Blush; and still later varieties—Red Baldwin
and King, Rhode Island Greening, Ben Davis, and Golden Russet. It has
been said that the "apple was king of the orchard, the strawberry queen of
the garden." At North Union and at many other Shaker societies the sisters
worked hard in their kitchens to turn the bountiful harvest of orchard and
garden into preserves, jams and jellies for home use and for sale.

Apple Parings Jelly

4 quarts apple parings and cores
4 cups water
5 cups sugar (variable)

Add water to freshly cut peels and cores, and simmer until fruit is soft.
Place into a jelly bag, and let hang to drain. DO NOT SQUEEZE. Measure juice into an enameled, glass or stainless steel saucepan and to each
cup of juice, add 1 cup sugar. Stir well, and boil rapidly until mixture jells
on a metal spoon. Be sure to test after 15 minutes and frequently after that,
so mixture does not crystallize. Pour into hot, sterilized jelly glasses immediately and seal. Makes about 5 cups.

Amelia's Shaker Recipes

SKILLED ORCHARDISTS: The Shakers were famous orchardists; they cultivated several new species of apples, among which were the quince apple and
a sweet variety which was especially adapted to drying and was used in their
applesauce. Their fruit was the best obtainable; they cultivated their orchards
and fertilized their trees thoroughly, and they trimmed their trees of all
excess wood buds, which caused them to bear very heavily.

Carrot Marmalade

3 cups carrots
Grated rind and juice of 2 lemons
Grated rind and juice of 1 large
  orange
6 cups sugar

Simmer carrots until tender, but still crisp. Drain well and chop finely with a knife or quickly process in a food processor, but not a grinder. Add the remaining ingredients and cook slowly for about 30 minutes, until it jells on a spoon. Test after 20 minutes, frequently after that. Skim surface foam. Pour into hot, sterilized jelly glasses or jars immediately, and seal.

Sister Mildred, Sabbathday Lake

Cranberry Preserves

4 cups cranberries
2 seedless oranges
2 cups hot water
1 cup seedless raisins
4 cups sugar
1 cup chopped walnuts or pecans

Grind raw cranberries and unpeeled oranges together. Add hot water and simmer until fruit is tender. Add raisins and sugar. Simmer slowly until conserve thickens. Add nuts and pour into hot, sterilized jars immediately, and seal. Makes about 5 cups.

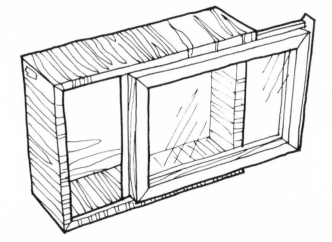

Bee box of tiger maple with sliding glass door; used to trap and carry the queen bee; from Enfield, Connecticut.

ABUNDANT CRANBERRIES: Cranberries grew in great profusion along Doan Brook, which flowed through the Shaker properties at North Union. Many recipes have been found in Shaker household journals for cranberry dumplings, puddings, sauces, tarts, cobblers, pies, relishes and even catsup. The Shakers also dried great quantities of them.

NORTH UNION IN 1848:   Elder Daniel Boler of New Lebanon wrote of North Union after a visit, "These Shakers are in comfortable circumstances. It is true that their land is not of the best for farm purposes for it is a stiff, heavy clay which makes all their work doubly hard; but on the other hand they have produced a famous growth of timber and have splendid orchards and mulberry groves."

Remove skins and cook pulp of grapes until soft. Press through a colander to remove seeds. Combine pulp, skins, sugar, raisins, juice and orange rind. Simmer slowly until thickened. Remove from heat and add nuts. Pour into hot, sterilized jars immediately, and seal. Makes about 4 pints.

Sister Lisset, North Union

Cube tomatoes. Place in a non-metallic or stainless steel bowl and sprinkle with salt. Let stand overnight. Rinse quickly and drain thoroughly. Place in an enameled, glass or stainless steel saucepan and add lemon, sugar and spices. Simmer for 2 hours. Pour immediately into hot, sterilized jars and seal. For a crystal-clear preserve, oil of spices, available at most drugstore chains and shops specializing in baking and candymaking supplies, may be used.

Sister Annie Bell, Canterbury

Wipe ALL the "fuzz" from the peaches. Split peaches into halves and remove stones. Do not peel. Crack about ¼ of the peach stones and remove kernels. Crush. Pack peach halves in layers in a large crockery or glass jug and sprinkle with crushed kernels. Add water, cover (not tightly) and place in a water bath over low heat for 4 to 5 hours. Pour the contents of the jug into a jelly bag and let hang to drain juice. DO NOT SQUEEZE. Measure juice into an enameled, glass or stainless steel saucepan and add lemon juice. For each cup of juice, add 1 cup sugar, and simmer until it is thickened and slides from the metal spoon. Test after 15 minutes and frequently after that. Pour into hot, sterilized jelly glasses immediately and seal. Makes about 5 cups.

This is a painstaking process but the result is delicious. The crushed kernel adds tremendously to the flavor. This recipe can be used for sour cherries, wild cherries or plums with equal success. If wild cherries are used, grind ⅓ of the stemmed cherries with their pits; this gives the jell a delicious, pungent flavor. Excellent served with venison or wild fowl.

Union Village

Grape Conserves

8 pounds Concord grapes
8 pounds sugar
1½ pounds seedless raisins
Rind of 4 oranges, grated
Juice from 4 oranges
1½ cups chopped pecans or walnuts

Green Tomato Preserves

12 medium green tomatoes
3 tablespoons salt
2 lemons, thinly sliced
2 cups brown sugar
1 teaspoon ground cloves
1 teaspoon ground nutmeg
1 teaspoon ground allspice

Sister Lettie's Peach Jelly

6 pounds ripe peaches
1 cup water
Juice of 2 lemons
Sugar (variable)

Strawberry Jam

8 cups sugar
2 cups water
4 pounds strawberries

Pick over and hull strawberries. Wash thoroughly and pat off excess water with a dry towel. Let air dry. Place sugar in a preserving kettle or in an enameled, glass or stainless steel saucepan and add water. Simmer to 230°F or until the syrup formed "strings" off the spoon. Remove from heat. Add fruit and let stand 10 minutes. Strain off the berries in a colander and set aside. Cook syrup again until it "strings" from the spoon. Again add fruit and let stand in syrup 10 minutes. Repeat process once more. Drain berries, reserving syrup. Reduce syrup to ½ of its volume and add fruit. Let stand 24 hours, covered with 4 layers of cheesecloth. Simmer gently for 15 minutes, pour into hot, sterilized jelly glasses immediately and seal. Makes about 4 pints.

Amelia's Shaker Recipes

Tomato Figs

8 pounds small, firm, ripe plum
   tomatoes
3 pounds brown sugar

Drop tomatoes into boiling water. Simmer for 2 minutes. Drain immediately and plunge into cold water. Slip off and discard skins. Place tomatoes in an enameled, glass or stainless steel saucepan and cover with sugar. Let stand 2 hours. Simmer slowly in their own juices until tomatoes look translucent, about 25 minutes. Check after 15 minutes and frequently after that. Do not cook too long, nor stir, nor break the tomatoes. Remove from kettle and place on a shallow cookie sheet that has a non-stick surface. Place a sheet of wax paper or plasticized freezer paper over the tomatoes and then a weighted or heavy platter on top to flatten tomatoes. Let stand 2 hours. Remove platter and paper and cover with syrup in which tomatoes were cooked. Store, covered with cheesecloth in a cool, dry place for about 7 days. Every 24 hours sprinkle with finely granulated sugar and dry for about 2 hours in an oven that has been heated to 140°F. The last day, sprinkle with sugar and pack into flat, moisture-proof boxes to store.

South Union

Shaker Tomato Jam

4 pounds ripe tomatoes
8 pounds sugar
Grated rind and juice of 4 oranges
Grated rind and juice of 8 lemons
3 sticks cinnamon

Drop tomatoes into boiling water. Simmer for 2 minutes. Remove skins and discard them. Finely chop tomatoes and add remaining ingredients. Place in an enameled, glass or stainless steel saucepan and simmer slowly until it jells on a spoon, 35 to 45 minutes. Test after 20 minutes and frequently after that. Skim surface foam. Pour into hot sterilized jelly glasses or jars immediately, and seal. Makes about 4 pints. This makes a most appetizing, shocking-pink confection.

PICKLES

The Center Family Broom Shop,
North Union, Ohio

PICKLES

Neither eat nor drink in haste and carefully avoid making any noises while eating.
– Gentle Manners.

On reading the handwritten annals on Shaker food, it seems the thrifty sisters pickled or preserved most anything, from the first tiny cucumber and pale shallot to the late seckel pear and the last frostbitten green tomato. Enormous crocks were filled with "Pickled Lily"—a combination of various chopped vegetables, spices and vinegars. Others contained stuffed peppers or mangoes for which there was a tremendous demand in February and March in the Cleveland markets. Translucent watermelon rind, lush spiced peaches and delicious little red crab apples steeped in their richly seasoned juices filled innumerable crocks in the great deep cellars of the Shakers. Not a bean or a gooseberry went to waste on these vast Shaker farms where from two to six families, ranging from 30 to 100 persons, were served three square meals daily for 365 days of the year. And, of course, there were many wayfarers who sought food at these hospitable gates as well as visiting ministries from other Shaker communities, who often stayed for several weeks at a time.

The sisters, preparing food for these large households, realized how these condiments and pickles dressed up simple fare and added needed variety to their limited winter and spring diet. Moreover, vinegar was the great preservative of food in the days before refrigeration. Living chiefly on what they raised, the Shakers needed to store food for months ahead. Pickles fit the Shakers' needs nicely.

Processing Pickled and Preserved Foods

The hot water bath canner is recommended for tomatoes and acid fruits which may be processed safely at boiling temperatures.

A cover is necessary to keep the water at a rolling boil during the processing. Wash jars and lids in hot detergent and water. Rinse thoroughly in hot water before starting. Fill jar to ½ inch from the top with food to be processed.

Be sure canner is deep enough so that boiling water will cover the tops of the jars by 1 inch. Allow space for expansion and boiling. In addition, a

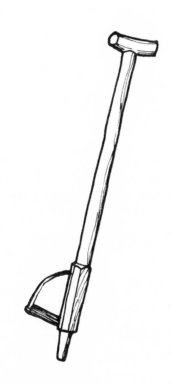

Hole digger for planting corn. Wood, with iron brace.

rack should be used which will hold the jars at least ½ inch from the bottom.

The pressure container is recommended for other vegetables, meats, poultry and other low-acid or neutral foods. Follow the manufacturer's recommended operating instructions.

The open kettle container is recommended for jams, jellies, preserves, relishes and some pickles.

Cook food in an uncovered saucepan or canning kettle. Then pour the food, boiling hot, into hot, sterilized jars. Jelly glasses or half-pint jars with two-piece tops may be used. The jelly glasses require sealing with hot paraffin.

Jars, jelly glasses and two-piece covers may be sterilized by, first, washing them in hot, soapy water, and rinsing well. Next, they may then be submerged in cold water and boiled, covered, at a rolling boil for 15 minutes. The heat may then be turned off and the jars and closures left in the water until ready to fill. Be sure to use tongs to remove them from the water. When in doubt, follow the manufacturer's directions for sterilizing lids and other closures.

Corn Relish

2 cups onions
2 cups ripe tomatoes
2 cups cucumbers
2 cups cut corn
2 cups cabbage
2 cups sugar
1½ teaspoons salt
1½ teaspoons celery salt
½ teaspoon turmeric
2 cups cider vinegar

Remove skins from onions and tomatoes and hard ends from cucumbers. Coarsely chop all vegetables and mix together. Combine remaining ingredients and add to vegetables. Place all in an enameled, glass or stainless steel saucepan and simmer for 20 minutes. Place into hot, sterilized jars immediately and seal. Makes about 4 pints.

North Union

Cranberry Relish

2 seedless oranges
2 cups cranberries
3 sour apples, cored
2 cups fresh pineapple pieces
2 cups sugar

Remove peel from one orange and discard. Place fruit into food processor to coarsely cut, or process through the coarse blade of a food grinder. Remove to a non-metallic or stainless steel bowl and refrigerate for 6 hours before using. Do not cook or peel fruits (except pineapple). For an interesting variation, add walnuts to fruit before processing. Makes about 1 quart.

Sweet Pickled Fruit

7 pounds whole crab apples, seckel
  pears or firm, small plums
7 cups sugar
2 quarts cider vinegar
4 cinnamon sticks
6 tablespoons whole cloves, cassia or
  allspice

If crab apples or plums are used, wash but do not peel. If pears are used, peel, but leave on stems. In an enameled or stainless steel saucepan, combine sugar, vinegar and spices and boil 5 minutes. Add fruit and cook slowly until fruit is tender but still crisp. Remove from heat, cover, and let stand in syrup overnight, or about 12 hours, to cool. Drain off syrup and simmer it until it becomes the consistency of honey, or is reduced to about ⅓ of its original volume. Pack fruit in hot, sterilized jars, cover with boiling syrup and seal at once. Makes about 6 pints.

Mary Whitcher's Shaker House-Keeper

Gooseberry Catsup

2 quarts gooseberries
4 cups sugar
1 teaspoon salt
1 tablespoon ground cinnamon
1 tablespoon ground cloves
1 teaspoon pepper
1 cup cider vinegar

Cut both stem and blossom ends from gooseberries with a small scissors. Mix seasonings and spices with vinegar and bring to a boil in an enameled, glass or stainless steel saucepan. Add berries and simmer until thickened. Pour into hot, sterilized jars immediately, and seal. Delicious with ham. Makes about 2 pints.

NOTE: Cranberries may be used in place of gooseberries for a delicious variation.

Union Village

DIRECTIONS FOR MAKING CRISP PICKLES: The North Union Shakers suggested throwing small cucumber pickles in a vat of brine strong enough "to float an egg." After a week pour off the brine and rinse pickles well. Place the pickles in large crocks and cover with the best vinegar; let stand for a couple of weeks longer. Then turn them into a brass cauldron with a goodly lump of alum and let them scald slowly over a very low heat. By no means let them come to a boil. They will now be a lovely green, and firm as well. Now add onions, horseradish, green and red peppers or anything that suits your taste. In packing away in crocks, scatter leaves among the layers and cover the top with these same leaves. This will prevent the pickles from softening.

SHAKERS AND SPICES: In the early days the Shakers ground all their spices at home by means of spice mills. If mills were not available, they were ground in a metal mortar or bruised and crushed with a cleaver. In these ways the greatest amount of goodness was obtained from these precious substances.

Pickled Grapes

8 pounds half-ripened grapes;
    Concord or Catawba are best
4 pounds brown sugar
2 quarts wine vinegar
½ cup whole cloves
½ cup whole allspice
½ cup cinnamon sticks

Wash thoroughly and pick grapes from stems. Tie spices in a cheesecloth bag. Place sugar and vinegar in a stainless steel, glass or enameled pot and add bag of spices. Bring to a boil, reduce heat and simmer until it has evaporated to at least half of its original volume. Pack grapes into hot, sterilized jars. Pour hot syrup over them and seal immediately. Makes about 6 pints.

This pickle is an excellent condiment when used with ham or poultry.

Amelia's Shaker Recipes

Pickled Onions

2 quarts very small white onions
1 quart milk
1 quart water
1 quart cider vinegar
1 tablespoon brown sugar
⅛ cup fresh grated horseradish
1 teaspoon pickling spice

Peel onions and simmer in mixture of milk and water in an enameled, glass or stainless steel saucepan until they are transparent, tender, but still firm and crisp. In another saucepan of the same kind, place vinegar, sugar, horseradish and spice and bring to a boil. Boil 3 minutes. Drain onions, discard liquid and pour the hot vinegar mixture over them. Let stand until cool enough to refrigerate. May by used, as is, when they are thoroughly chilled. Keep in the refrigerator. Makes 8 pints.

Sister Marguerite, Canterbury

THE NORTH UNION VINEYARDS: Like many Shaker communities, North Union had extensive vineyards. There were large packing and warehouses on the premises and the Lake Shore Railroad passed through the property. Tons of grapes were packed and shipped both east and west from the warehouses. Other great quantities were made into medicinal wines, wine vinegar, grape juice, catsup, spiced grapes, and Concord grape pie.

Late varieties of grapes, such as Catawbas, which withstood the light frosts and were harvested late, had their stems sealed with beeswax and were packed in sawdust to be used at Thanksgiving.

AN ELDRESS ADVISES ON PICKLES: Eldress Clymena Miner suggested, "If you wish plump pickles, fill your large pickling kettle half full of small cucumbers (2 inches in length), and then fill the kettle almost to the top with cold water. Put on the stove and heat almost to the boiling point. Pour off the water immediately and refill with cold water. Do this nine times and you will not have wilted, shrunken pickles. If you wish crisp pickles, add a lump of alum to the last water. Spice your vinegar to suit your taste and pour on hot."

Pickled Peaches

Wash thoroughly and wipe all the fuzz from peaches. Insert 3 cloves into each. Tie the remaining spices in a cheescloth bag. Place sugar and vinegar in a stainless steel or enameled or glass saucepan with spice bag and boil 10 minutes. Pour syrup while very hot over peaches. Remove from heat, cover and let stand 24 hours. Repeat twice more, draining syrup and heating to a boil each time. The fourth day, scald the fruit in the syrup, by heating to the boiling point, and holding it there for 3 minutes. Pack into hot, sterilized jars and seal immediately. Makes about 6 pints.

Amelia's Shaker Recipes

7 pounds firm, ripe peaches
¼ cup whole cloves
¼ cup cinnamon sticks, broken
¼ cup whole allspice
8 cups sugar
1 quart cider vinegar

Shaker Cut Pickles

Wash and cut cucumbers into chunks. Do not peel. Add salt to boiling water and pour over cucumbers. Remove from heat and let stand covered overnight to cool. Make a syrup of vinegar, water, sugar and spices by cooking all together until it evaporates to half of its original volume. Drain pickles and add to hot syrup. Return to heat and bring to a rolling boil. Pack into hot, sterilized jars and fill with remaining syrup. Seal at once. Makes 1 gallon.

South Union

4 quarts medium-size cucumbers
½ cup salt
Boiling water
3 cups cider vinegar
1 cup water
2 cups sugar
1 teaspoon dry mustard
1 teaspoon whole allspice
1 teaspoon celery seed
1 teaspoon mustard seed
1 teaspoon turmeric

ELIJAH THE PRUNER: The origins and success of all six of the old orchards in the Valley of God's Pleasure was due to the devotion of Elijah Russell, North Union's head horticulturist. He was a skilled pruner and grafter, and sometimes would graft different varieties of fruit scions to various trees. A visiting elder recalled discovering a plum tree which looked just like a peach tree, but was loaded with plums: "Elder Brother [Elijah] said it was one of the best bearers in this part of the country; it hardly ever missed a season. He said it bore a very rich fruit—especially good for preserves."

Spiced Vinegar

2 ounces whole black pepper
1 ounce fresh ginger root
5 cups cider vinegar
1 ounce whole allspice
1 ounce salt
½ teaspoon cayenne (optional)

Bruise the black pepper and ginger root, to extract more of the flavor, by wrapping them in a napkin and hitting them sharply with the flat side of a chef's knife or the bottom of a small skillet. Mix all ingredients together and place in an enameled, glass or stainless steel pot. Simmer slowly for about 30 minutes to extract flavors from spices. Strain through several layers of cheesecloth. Use instead of plain vinegar in any pickle recipe. Makes 1 quart.

Watermelon Rind Pickle

7 pounds watermelon rind
2½ quarts water
⅓ cup salt
6½ cups brown sugar
2 cups cider vinegar
1 cup water
1 tablespoon whole cloves
2 cinnamon sticks
2 lemons

Peel melon rind and cut into one-inch squares. Place in a large bowl. Mix salt with water and pour over the rind. Refrigerate for 3 days. Drain and replace water with fresh, cold water for one hour. Simmer together, sugar, vinegar, 1 cup water and spices until it is reduced to ½ of the original volume. Slice the lemon into paper-thin slices. Do not remove rind. Place melon and lemon into hot syrup and boil until watermelon is clear, about 35 to 45 minutes. Use the "open kettle" method of processing. Ladle pickle evenly into hot, sterilized jars and fill with remaining hot syrup. Seal at once. Makes about 6 pints.

South Union

GATHER UP THE FRAGMENTS

The East Family Broom Shop,
North Union, Ohio

GATHER UP THE FRAGMENTS

You must be prudent, and saving of every good thing which God blesses you with, so that you may have wherewith to give to them that stand in need. – Mother Ann Lee.

The story is told of how on one fine Saturday morning in August, 1782, Mother Ann and the elders, with a large company of Believers, set out from the Goodrich home at Hancock, Massachusetts, to visit New Lebanon, New York. They arrived at Israel Talcott's place shortly before noon and saw that Abigail Talcott had her pot of meat and vegetables over the fire preparing dinner for her little family. Mother Ann spoke to Abigail, saying, "We have need of food; you must feed us, Abigail, and all who are with us."

Eyeing the crowd of nearly forty persons, the dismayed Abigail exclaimed, "But I must cook more meat and sauce."

But Mother Ann responded, "Nay! There is plenty!"

When Abigail served her dinner, all the company sat down, ate and were amply satisfied. She was astonished that so many could be fed by so little. The story concludes: "At the meeting which followed so great was the manifestation of the power of God and so clear the evidence of the testimony that every mouth was stopped!"

It was said that this miraculous feeding was often repeated when Mother Ann and her followers traveled through the countryside gathering in converts. Whatever their literal truth, stories like these remind us of how the Shakers always found nature bountiful, even when others could not. "Every day is Thanksgiving Day at the Shaker communities," a North Union elder once remarked.

Thrifty use of what they had was one way the Shakers assured themselves of nature's bounty. In her youth Mother Ann had seen the hunger of the poor in the rapidly growing mill city of Manchester; it led her to abhor waste of all kinds. She and her followers laid down strict rules on the matter, such as: "Nothing edible is to be left upon the plate when a Shaker has finished his meal." A Shaker could help himself as often as he wished so long as he ate what he had taken. The rules applied to visitors as well. Lest there be any misunderstanding, a set of printed rules was posted in the dining halls. The Table Monitor, as the set of rules was called, was written by Sister Hannah Bronson, a native of Vermont who entered the Mt. Lebanon community in 1800.

The term "Shaker your plate" came into common use, meaning to finish everything in one's dish and take no more food than one could eat. The Shakers knew that there are always people needing food; their hospitality to the hungry in an age before widespread public assistance was well known. Elder Matthew Houston of North Union wrote to the Ministry at Mt. Lebanon: "Daily there are demands made upon us for food. Due to the bad weather there is a grave shortage of wheat in these parts; this means that many are hungry. So far we have not sent away any without bread...."

For economy's sake, Shakers salvaged all edible greens, pot liquors, skins of fruit and peels of vegetables, thereby gleaning valuable nutrition in the process. They used the bones and trimmings of meat, fish and fowl for broth in reinforcing stews, gravies and soups. They made excellent use of all leftovers as well: excess milk was made into cheese, and when certain recipes called for large quantities of egg yolks, the Shakers immediately concocted dishes which used up the corresponding egg whites. They took minute care in storing food, and their household journals are filled with warnings: "Ventilate your storage places and cellars well....Constantly watch the brine on your pickle....Assort your apples frequently, for one bad one will contaminate the whole barrel."

However, the Shakers were concerned with more than just using food wisely and preparing it well; they also sought to make meals pleasant times by teaching proper manners at the table. In a little manual on manners published in 1823, the Shakers advised, "It is necessary at table that we consider the happiness of those about us, therefore a system of rules must be observed during the time occupied at table in order to make it a pleasurable satisfaction as well as a physical necessity.

"Remember that a slight deviation from the rules of good manners at table may offend those about us so that the meal becomes an occasion of pain instead of pleasure....Keep your arms near your body—never on the table. Also be careful to have your feet directly in front of your own chair, never in the way of others.

"Our lives are primarily for the purpose of giving pleasure to others, to those about us, therefore we must practice orderliness and cleanliness—without which we are not worthy of the name gentleman or Christian."

And so it was that even in such ordinary matters as cooking and eating that the Shakers demonstrated qualities of thrift, precision, simplicity, devotion, grace, and compassion that continue to impress and inspire their fellow Americans to this day.

In an age which some find troublesome for its meaninglessness, fragmentation and alienation, we can envy the Shaker's ability to integrate the small and the large, the mundane and the glorious, in one seamless whole. Their view was expressed a century ago in *The Manifesto:*

"When we Americans learn the great lesson that all Life is a Unit; that the physical, intellectual and spiritual are all One Life and that whatever mars one phase of it mars the whole—we will be better off."

Corner cupboard, made in two pieces: poplar for the bottom and tulip for the top. Used by the Shakers at North Union, the two pieces were sold at the dispersal auction in 1889 and later donated separately to the Shaker Historical Society.

THE SHAKER HISTORICAL SOCIETY

The Shaker Historical Society was organized in the fall of 1947 to preserve the heritage of both the Shakers and the Shaker Heights area from pioneer days to the present. The Society carries on an active program, including classes and tours for adults and children, membership meetings, the marking of historic sites and library artifacts, and maintenance of a library and museum of articles and records of the Shakers and Warrensville Township. New members are welcome; details on membership may be obtained by writing the Society.

The Shaker Museum is not housed in a Shaker building – none are left – but in a 1910 mansion, one of those built in the era of the Van Sweringens, the enterprising young brothers who developed the "garden city suburb" of Shaker Heights. Appropriately overlooking Upper Shaker Lake, the museum is located in the vicinity of the Center Family, most of whose main buildings were situated on nearby Lee Road. The Museum's front lawn was part of the Center Family's apple orchard, and the old Shaker vegetable garden was at the rear. The Museum itself houses a collection of Shaker artifacts from North Union and other societies, and periodically also features special exhibits.

The Museum building also houses the Nord Library of local history and the Spirit Tree, a museum gift shop.

The Women's Committee was founded in 1971 as an autonomous group whose members devote time and effort to promoting the Society's objectives. By means of fund-raising projects they have purchased many Shaker artifacts and paid for a number of needed repairs to Museum property. They welcome members.

THE SHAKER HISTORICAL SOCIETY
16740 South Park Boulevard
Shaker Heights, Ohio 44120
(216) 921-1201

Museum hours: 2-4 p.m. Tuesday through Friday and 2-5 p.m. Sundays.

The Shaker Historical Society Building

CONTRIBUTORS

Caroline (Behlen) Piercy wrote the original version of the present book, published in 1953 under the title, *The Shaker Cook Book: Not by Bread Alone.* Born in Cleveland in 1886, she married Shaker Heights physician Harry D. Piercy in 1916. Mrs. Piercy was the moving force in founding the Shaker Historical Society in Shaker Heights. She wrote several books about the Shakers, and, with her husband, contributed several rooms of furniture to the Western Reserve Historical Society. She died in 1955.

Arthur P. Tolve, co-author, substantially revised and updated the recipes and instructions in Mrs. Piercy's book. A member of the home economics faculty of Bowling Green State University, where he teaches courses in restaurant and institutional food service management, he worked for a number of years in estate catering, banquet management, and dietetics. He was chair of the Department of Food Service Management at the New York Food and Hotel Management School from 1974 to 1981. He is co-author (with James H. Bissland III) of *Sister Jennie's Shaker Desserts* (Bowling Green, Ohio: Gabriel's Horn Publishing Co., 1983); of *Standardizing Foodservice for Quality and Efficiency* (Westport, Connecticut: AVI Publishing Co., 1984), and of a computer program (written in Applesoft/Basic): *Recipe Modification and Adjustment.*

Patricia J. Forgac, whose drawings of the Shaker buildings and artifacts illustrate the text and back cover of this book, is heritage director and assistant city planner for the city of Shaker Heights. She has graduate degrees in architecture and business administration from Kent State University, and is a trustee of the Shaker Historical Society.

Kathy Jakobsen, one of America's foremost folk artists, is a native of Michigan. Her work is in a number of books, museums and private collections.

Lynn Hostetler, a graphic designer in Bowling Green, Ohio, designed this book and supervised its printing. She teaches in the School of Art at Bowling Green State University and was formerly art director for the University's public relations and publications office.

James H. Bissland III, Ph.D., general editor, is an associate professor in the School of Journalism, Bowling Green State University. He has been personally acquainted with the Shakers since childhood, when his parents were frequent visitors to the communities formerly at Mt. Lebanon, New York, and Hancock, Massachusetts.

FOR MORE INFORMATION

If you would like to get better acquainted with the Shakers and their culinary arts, there are a variety of opportunities: two Shaker societies continue to exist, a number of fine museums display the artifacts of the Believers, and – most deliciously of all – there are several ways to taste the Shaker past.

As they have since the 1790s, Shakers continue to live at Canterbury, New Hampshire (a few miles north of Concord), and at Sabbathday Lake, Maine (between Portland and Lewiston). Open to visitors during the regular tourist season, both communities offer walking tours, exhibits showing how the Shakers lived – and the strong possibility that you will meet a Shaker or two. More information is available from Shaker Village, Canterbury, New Hampshire 03244, and the United Society of Shakers, Sabbathday Lake, Poland Spring, Maine 04274.

Herbs represent one of the oldest Shaker industries. The Shakers at Sabbathday Lake are still in the herb business, and offer by mail "A Catalogue of Shaker Teas, Culinary Herbs, Herbal Books, Potpourri, and Other Interesting Items" in return for a self-addressed, stamped envelope.

Elsewhere, two Shaker museum villages are famed for their dining delights. One is Shakertown at Pleasant Hill, Kentucky (25 miles southwest of Lexington), which not only preserves 27 original buildings of that community, occupied by Shakers from 1806 to 1910, but also offers lodging in the same rooms where Shakers once retired, as well as dining on "abundant Kentucky country fare" in the Trustees' Office Inn. Write Shakertown at Pleasant Hill, 3500 Lexington Road, Harrodsburg, Kentucky 40330; telephone (606) 734-5411.

Another treasure of a museum village is Hancock Shaker Village, near Pittsfield in western Massachusetts. Hancock, where Shakers lived from 1790 to 1960, offers 20 original buildings, including the famed 1826 Round Stone Barn. Special workshops and educational programs are also offered at Hancock, which is open during the tourist season. Hancock was restored under the leadership of Amy Bess Miller. While Hancock offers a lunch shop and the "Good Room," where homemade food products such as baked goods and preserves are sold, the culinary high points of the season are the famed food festivals usually held early each August: the Kitchen Festival, an educational program of cooking demonstrations (with results you can sample), and the World's People's Dinners, which are Shaker-style meals in the Believers' dining room (and for which early reservations are recommended). For more information, write Hancock Shaker Village, Box 898, Pittsfield, Massachusetts; telephone (413) 443-0188.

For dining in a country inn enhanced by a number of Shaker relics, travelers should consider the Golden Lamb, billed as Ohio's oldest inn, and located in Lebanon, only five miles from the site of the Shaker society at Union Village (1805-1910) in southwestern Ohio. A collection of pieces of Shaker furniture and other artifacts can be found here; ask to be seated in the Shaker dining room. Still more Shaker items can be found in the Warren County Historical Society Museum, only a few steps from the Golden Lamb.

There are, of course, a number of other fine museums in which relics of the Shaker domestic and other arts can be seen. Some of these are the Shaker Museum at Old Chatham, New York (20 miles southeast of Albany); the Henry Francis DuPont Winterthur Museum in Delaware (tour reservations required); Shakertown at South Union, Kentucky (where several buildings are preserved); the Fruitlands Museums in Harvard, Massachusetts, where a beautifully restored Shaker House is one of several museums set in a breathtaking location; and the Kettering-Moraine Museum near Dayton, Ohio. Some, such as the museum at Old Chatham, South Union and Kettering-Moraine have festivals most summers during which good, homemade food – some from Shaker recipes – is available.

And, for those who wish to create their own Shaker taste experience, there are cookbooks. Strongly recommended is *The Best of Shaker Cooking,* by Amy Bess Miller (president of the Hancock museum) and Persis Fuller. This is both an encyclopedic collection of recipes from many Shaker kitchens and an extensive history of Shaker food and cooking. And fond memories of dining at Pleasant Hill, Kentucky, can be kept alive through two collections of recipes from that museum village's kitchens: *We Make You Kindly Welcome* and *Welcome Back to Pleasant Hill,* both by Elizabeth C. Kremer, long the director of Pleasant Hill's food operations.

Finally, the most effective way to keep up with the fascinating – and ever-changing – world of Shaker is to subscribe to *The Shaker Messenger,* a quarterly magazine published by Diana and Paul Van Kolken, Box 45, Holland, Michigan 49423.

GLOSSARY

Modern cookery terms used in *The Shaker Cookbook* are included here to help the reader obtain best results.

Bake: To cook by enclosed heat and constant temperature.

Baste: To moisten surface of food to keep it from drying and to add flavor.

Beat: To mix or stir vigorously with spoon, whisk, or beater.

Blanch: To submerge food in boiling liquid or hot fat for a short time.

Blend: To mix two or more ingredients until smooth.

Boil: To submerge food in boiling liquid to thoroughly cook.

To Bone: To remove bones, usually from raw meats, fish, poultry.

Braise: To brown food pieces first, then cook in a small amount of liquid.

To Bread: To coat food with bread or cracker crumbs.

Broil: To cook by direct heat, either over or under the source of heat.

Brown: To brown surface of food, either in a pan with fat or by direct heat.

To Candy: Cook in heavy syrup until transparent, then dry out slightly to glaze.

Chop: To cut into small pieces.

Coat: To cover food or coat it, usually with flour.

Combine: To mix two or more ingredients together.

Core: To remove the seed section from top to bottom of fruit.

To Cream: To beat fat and sugar, or fat alone, until fluffy and creamy.

To Cube: To cut into cube shapes.

Cut In: To work or combine solid fat with dry ingredients usually by knives (scissors fashion), wire blender or whisk.

Deglaze: To add stock, water or wine to particles stuck on surface of pan, reducing to half original volume.

Dice: To cut into small cubes.

Dot: To scatter bits of fat over entire surface of food to be cooked.

Dredge: To coat with flour prior to frying, braising, or roasting.

Drizzle: To pour melted fat or other liquid in a thin stream.

Dust: To cover food lightly with flour, sugar, etc.

Fillet: The boneless, skinless side of a fish.

Flake: To dig into food with fork(s) to separate particles.

Fold: A gentle up-and-over motion, moving food from the bottom up over onto the top.

Fry: To cook in half-inch of fat.

Garnish: To decorate food wth colorful and/or tangy bits of other foods.

To Glace: See *To Candy*.

Glazing: The coating of the surface of food with syrup until it glistens.

Grate: To scrape surface of food to remove the surface or skin.

Grind: To chop finely in a machine or grinder.

Infuse: To let substance stand in a warm place in hot liquid to extract flavor from substance into liquid.

Knead: To manipulate or work dough to incorporate air until texture is smooth.

Macerate: To gently press one or two substances together with a fork or spoon to allow blending and infusion of flavors.

Marinate: To soak or let stand in flavorful liquid to add flavor to the food.

Mash: To reduce to pulp, but not pulverize.

Mince: To chop finely with a knife.

Mix: To unite two or more ingredients.

Panning: To use small amount, no liquid, covering food in skillet to steam.

Parboil: To boil for short time to prepare for another cooking method.

Parcook: To cook by dry or moist heat for a short time to prepare for another cooking method.

Pare: To strip away outside layers.

Peel: To cut away skin a strip at a time.

Plumping: To soak dried fruits in warm water or other liquid until softened.

Poach: To slip into simmering liquid just to cover food.

Puree: To reduce to a smooth liquid, heavy with tiny particles of solids.

Render: To melt solid animal fats with gentle heat.

Roast: See *Bake.*

To Roll: To roll out with rolling pin, or roll up into a tight cylinder. Also see *Coat.*

Roux: A mixture of melted fat and flour.

Sauté: To cook in a small amount of fat in skillet at moderately high heat.

Scald: To bring up to temperatures slightly below boiling and then remove from heat.

Score: To make slits in surface of food.

Shred: To cut or rip into small thin slivers.

Sift: To agitate dry, powdered, or granular food through a mesh or screen.

Simmer: To cook in large amounts of liquid, below boiling point.

Steam: To cook in small amount of simmering liquid, not touching food, using covered utensil.

Steep: See *Infuse.*

Stew: To simmer food in small amount of liquid.

Stir: To mix with circular motion with spoon, or machine on slow speed.

Strain: To pass food through cloth, strainer or sieve to remove particles.

Toss: To mix by gently turning bulky ingredients over and over.

Truss: To skewer and tie fowl into compact shape before cooking.

Velouté: A white sauce made with meat, fish or poultry stock as the liquid.

Whip: To incorporate air by beating vigorously with whisk or at high speed on a machine.

INDEX TO RECIPES

To order additional copies of

THE
SHAKER
COOKBOOK

*Recipes and Lore from
the Valley of God's Pleasure*

Send $14.95 plus $3 for UPS delivery

GABRIEL'S HORN PUBLISHING CO.
Department S
P.O. Box 141
Bowling Green, Ohio 43402
Telephone 1-800-235-4676

Gabriel's Horn Publishing Co.
Dept. S
P.O. Box 141
Bowling Green, Ohio 43402

Please send _____ copies of THE SHAKER COOKBOOK AT $17.95 ppd. to:

Name _____

Address _____

City _____ State _____ Zip _____
Ohio orders should include 6 % sales tax.

ABOUT THIS BOOK:

The main text of *The Shaker Cookbook* is set in
11/13 Goudy Old Style, keystroked on Apple IIe micro-
computers in Bowling Green, Ohio, and sent in "elec-
tronic manuscript" form to Huron Valley Graphics,
Inc., Ann Arbor, Michigan. Type was set by Huron
Valley Graphics on Linotron 202 phototypesetters using
DEC computers and the TEXT Ed composition system
developed by Edit Systems, Inc., a subsidiary of Huron
Valley Graphics. Chapter titles and cover copy was set
in Goudy Old Style by the House of Type, Toledo,
Ohio. The book was printed on 60 lb. Booktext by
BookCrafters, Inc., Chelsea, Michigan.